Strange Lights in West Texas

James Bunnell

Copyright © 2015 James Bunnell

All rights reserved. No part of this book may be reproduced or transmitted in any form or by any means, electronic or mechanical, including photocopying, recording or by any informational storage and retrieval system, without written permission from the author, except for the inclusion of brief quotations in a review.

Library of Congress Control Number: 2015911783

ISBN-978-0-9709249-7-1

Printed and bound in China

Lacey Publishing Company
Benbrook, Texas 76132
laceypub@gmail.com

Table of Contents

Acknowledgements 5

Introduction 7

Chapter 1   Marfa Mystery Lights: Accounts from Those Who Have Seen Them 15

Chapter 2   WHERE Are Those Lights? 31

Chapter 3   Visit the View Park! 47

Chapter 4   The Art of Rejecting Ordinary Lights 53

Chapter 5   FAQs 63

Chapter 6   Best Evidence for Mystery Lights 71

                 Feb. 19, 2003: First Capture of ML Details ... 74

                 May 7, 2003: Flight of Two Complex MLs ... 80

                 May 8, 2003: ML Explodes 89

                 May 8, 2004: Multiple MLs 94

                 Aug. 11, 2006: Shooting Over the Gate 101

                 Oct. 19, 2006: Red October 108

                 Jul, 23, 2007: A Wild Flight 122

Chapter 7   WHAT Are Those Lights? 131

Chapter 8   What Are They Not? 147

Chapter 9   Why Mystery Lights Are Important 157

Appendix: Automated Night Cameras **165**

References.. **173**

Acknowledgments

    I owe a special debt of gratitude to a remarkable group of Marfa ranch owners. Without them my investigation of Marfa Lights would not have been possible. These folks not only tolerated my many intrusions, but actively assisted my efforts in countless ways. What they did for my investigative effort is greatly appreciated.

    As I wrote in **Hunting Marfa Lights,** I am especially grateful to Kerr and Mary Belle Mitchell, whose steady support of my research effort made my long-term investigation possible. Kerr Mitchell not only tolerated my presence on his property, but actively assisted using his machinery, equipment, and skills to enable unique facilities that could not have been otherwise accomplished. I am also especially grateful to Richard and Robert Nunley who not only granted permission to be on their property, but accepted and tolerated my equipment and my many visits to their property. A special thanks goes to Bill Shurley who also accommodated my presence and equipment on his ranch. Early in my work, Kevin Webb relocated camera station Snoopy to a different ranch for me, something I could not have done alone.

    A very special thanks to my brother, Will Bunnell, who provided encouragement, comments and the electrical knowledge that assisted me throughout my investigation. I am also most grateful for joint investigations and collaboration with Dr. Karl Stephan and his smart students from Texas State University.

The Marfa Lights story would not be complete without the accounts of all the people who have published or otherwise shared their Marfa Lights stories, as published in **Hunting Marfa Lights,** plus story contributors to this book, in alphabetical order: Sandra Aguirre, Charlotte Allen, Joe Balderas, Bill and family, Maria Colfry, Dan and wife, Hollis and Linda Fuchs, Robert Grotty, Olga Landrum, James Nixon III, Lydia Quiroz, Linda Shaw and Dirk & Sarah Vander Zee. These stories are invaluable contributions that reveal the depth and complexity of Marfa Light experiences.

Last, but certainly not least, I wish to thank my wife, Dr. Sandra M. Dees, for her unflagging support of my investigation, for her skillful and always helpful editing of this manuscript, and for the many Marfa days and nights we shared working together as a team installing, improving, and maintaining nighttime monitoring equipment. We enjoyed many beautiful Texas nights together in our efforts to capture meaningful ML photographs and data.

James Bunnell, 2015

Figure 1. Marfa Lights View Park Pavilion at night.

Introduction

I am James Bunnell, a retired aerospace engineer. On two nights during the Thanksgiving holidays in the year 2000, my wife and I went looking for the fabled "Marfa Lights" that I remembered as a youth growing up in Presidio County. We got lucky: We were treated to incredible and, for us, mysterious light displays. Intrigued, I decided to return with a camera and do a short investigation. That "short" investigation took twelve years and resulted in three books that chronicled a search for meaningful answers. That investigation is now history. This fourth and final book provides my answers, my explanations of what they are, how to see them and why they are important.

These lights are called "Marfa Lights" because they have been showing up for at least the past century near a small Texas town by the name of Marfa, population less than 2000 (according to the Census in 2010). Marfa is situated in a basin surrounded by beautiful mountains that are sometimes called "foothills of the Rockies." Sixty miles south of Marfa is the border crossing between Presidio (USA) and Ojinaga (Mexico). Eighty miles southeast of Marfa is the Big Bend National Park. With an elevation of 4688 feet above sea level, Marfa is located in high desert of the Chihuahuan plateau, in the Trans-Pecos region of West Texas. It is the county seat of Presidio County. Marfa was established in 1881 as a water stop for the Texas-New Orleans railroad. MLs are most often seen nine miles east of town in a local region known as Mitchell Flat. Although there are several large ranches in that area now, the name comes from the pioneer family that was among the earliest to settle there.

Marfa has made a name for itself by being chosen as the filming location for three award-winning movies, **Giant, There will be Blood, and No Country for Old Men,** but it is best known nationally and internationally as the location of the Marfa Lights phenomena. These unusual lights are so famous that the State of Texas has built a unique roadside rest stop on the south side of Highway US 90, overlooking Mitchell Flat. This rest stop is also a "viewing station" specifically designed to accommodate the many light-hunting visitors who come every night of the year.

As a young boy, I grew up in Marfa and 60 miles south in Presidio. I was aware of these mysterious lights and knew where people were stopping on US 90 to see them. There was no View Park in those days but local people knew where to pull off the road to have a look, and the "Marfa Lights parking spot" was well worn by tire tracks. The best location was close to an old Army training base built during the Second World War. Primary training for bomber pilots was conducted at this airfield using twin engine Cessna AT-17 or UC-78 aircraft. Pilots called them "Bamboo Bombers" because of the amount of wood used in their construction (**Figure 2**). Many brave young men completed their primary training at the

Army airfield in Marfa and were then deployed to fly combat missions on behalf of our country (**Figure 3**).

When I retired and returned to my home state of Texas, the Army Airfield was long gone. The hangers my brother and I had played in so many years ago had vanished. Only broken foundations could be seen where buildings and hangers once stood. The long runways are still there, but you have to be aloft to see them; they are not visible from the ground. The worn parking spot I remembered from my youth had been replaced by a small, paved parking area and rest stop with picnic tables. The land was donated to the Texas Department of Transportation (TXDOT) by ranch owner Clayton Williams. The park provided a convenient place to safely pull off of US 90, park, and look for Marfa Lights. That small View Park was upgraded in 2003 with a donation of more land by Clayton Williams. The Texas Transportation Department substantially improved their expanded park by adding a pavilion with rest rooms and a viewing platform plus graveled trails leading to picnic tables and eight information plaques (**Map 1** and **1a**). These improvements greatly enhanced public convenience for both travelers and hunters of the fabled mystery lights.

On any given night, many people visit the Marfa Lights View Park hoping to see a genuine mystery light. The problem is that many different kinds of lights can be seen from the View Park. Looking in the wrong direction will bring into view mysterious-looking car lights. Looking in the right direction before you have located the "on-all-night" ranch lights in Mitchell Flat might cause you to mistake distant ranch lights, or ranch vehicles, for mystery lights. This difficulty has created both true believers and true skeptics when it comes to the Marfa Lights.

I have written this book for people who have open minds and are receptive to logical arguments supported by data. It is written for those who have not yet visited Marfa and might, or might not, consider doing so, as well as those who have visited and wish to better understand what they may have seen. It is also written for people worldwide who have an

Figure 2. "Cessna UC-78 Bobcat in Flight" by Unknown (http://www.flickr.com/photos/sdasmarchives/4559093205/in/photostream. Licensed under Public Domain via Wikimedia Commons - https://commons.wikimedia.org/wiki/File:Cessna_UC-78_Bobcat_in_flight).

Figure 3. Plaque attached to right wall of what once was the AAF entrance.

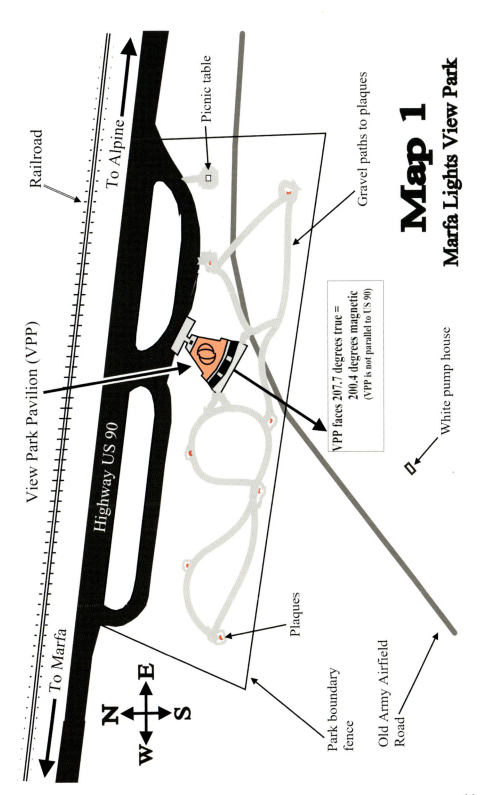

Map 1a: View Park Pavilion Detail

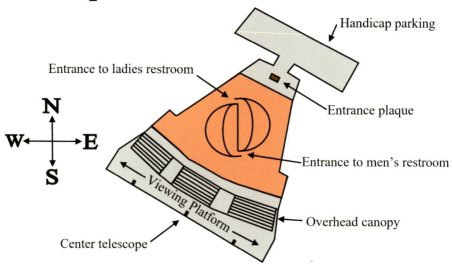

interest in mysterious lights of this type.

Marfa lights -- mysterious orbs in the night or just hype?

It is certainly true that many, and maybe most, people who visit Marfa looking for mysterious lights end up seeing explainable lights and may assume they are the mysterious lights that have made the town of Marfa so famous. But rest assured, there actually are mysterious lights (in this book I abbreviate "mysterious lights" and call them "MLs") that are sometimes seen east of Marfa.

MLs, in my experience, are rare, but very real, physical phenomena with nighttime displays that have fascinated observers throughout recorded history going all the way back to Native Americans who believed them to be stars that had fallen to earth. MLs are capable of remarkable behaviors and intriguing displays for visitors lucky enough to catch them in action. It is not often in today's modern world that one can observe physical phenomena that seem to defy conventional explanations as MLs do. People who have been fortunate enough to experience a good showing describe them using terms such as "striking," "unusual," "intriguing,"

MARFA MYSTERY LIGHTS

The Marfa Mystery Lights are visible on many clear nights between Marfa and Paisano Pass as one looks toward the Chinati Mountains. The lights may appear in various colors as they move about, split apart, melt together, disappear and reappear.

Robert Ellison, a young cowboy, reported sighting the lights in 1883. He spotted them while tending a herd of cattle and wondered if they were Apache Indian campfires.

Apache Indians believed these eerie lights to be stars dropping to the earth.

Many viewers have theories ranging from scientific to science fiction as they describe their ideas of aliens in UFO's, ranch house lights, St. Elmo's fire, or headlights from vehicles on US 67, the Presidio highway. Some believe the lights are an electrostatic discharge, swamp gases, moonlight shining on veins of mica, or ghosts of Conquistadors searching for gold.

An explanation as to why the lights cannot be located is an unusual phenomenon similar to a miracle, where atmospheric conditions produced by the interaction of cold and warm layers of air bend light so that it can be seen from afar, but not up close.

The mystery of these lights still remains unresolved.

Figure 4. Text taken from Plaque located at View Park entrance. Advice in the first sentence, "...as one looks toward the Chinati Mountains." is unfortunate because vehicle lights from north bound traffic on US 67 can be seen nightly in that direction.

"beautiful," "energetic," and "wonderful."

Simply stated, confusion over whether MLs are misidentification of explainable lights or something truly extraordinary stems from the fact that MLs are rare while vehicle lights, and other man-made lights, are common in today's world. It is not the case that MLs are only a myth. It is a myth that they are nothing more than misidentification of explainable lights. This book presents a strong case, supported by honest photography and investigative details, for the existence of uncommon and very unusual, but real physical phenomena happening in nighttime skies near Marfa, Texas, as well as many other places worldwide. They are more than just intriguing. They are natural phenomena in need of serious scientific study.

Chapter 1
Marfa Mystery Lights
Accounts From Those Who Have Seen Them

Figure 5. Southeast view from Marfa Lights View Park Pavilion viewing platform, 2003 shows the center telescope, a small white pump house, and the horizon profile of background mesas.

People Stories

There is no better introduction to Mysterious Lights (MLs) than stories told by those who have experienced the wonder and excitement of actually witnessing MLs in action. The website, www.marfatxlights.com, has provided a collection point for ML accounts from both residents and visitors to the Mitchell Flat area and a small sample of these are reproduced in this chapter, the "people stories." Boldface has been added by this author to direct special attention to particular comments.

Strange Lights (SL) Story #1

MLs are not always rare!
Time: 1968 - 1969
Email from Hollis and Linda Fuchs

My wife and I attended Sul Ross State University over 40 years ago and viewed Marfa Lights numerous times in the fall semester of 1968 and spring of 1969. In fact, I cannot remember a time we did not see them on a clear night when we were looking for them or when we stopped near the old Army Airfield as we were returning from El Paso at night. We also attended picture shows in Marfa from time to time and would stop and view Marfa Light (ML) activity when returning to Alpine. We probably never watched MLs much past 11 PM because of the curfew at the women's dorm. In those days, we watched from several locations, all within about a mile of the old Army Airfield where the Marfa Lights View Park is now located (nothing like that existed then).

The **MLs we observed were all located due south to southeast of where the View Park is now located.** We do not recall any association with thunderstorms. Vehicle traffic on Highway 67 (and US 90) was much less then, but we recognized that lights visible to the southwest were vehicle lights from northbound traffic on Highway 67. There were also occasional vehicle lights from ranch trucks traveling roads in Mitchell Flat.

The majority of MLs we saw were high fliers, anywhere from 1 to 5 degrees above the skyline. They were always white to bright yellow or yellow-orange. We never saw any other colors but did not have binoculars to watch them with. **They were unaffected by wind in any way.** They appeared in mid-air, often more than one, they divided, merged, went out, came back on, varied in brightness, traveled around, orbited or "danced" with one another -- made us think they were playing with one another. They were fun to watch. We also observed low flying MLs.

MLs always looked to be miles away, but there was no way to judge distance or to estimate their actual size. We do not recall seeing one illuminate the ground or surrounding vegetation. I did not get any impression that combustion or ignition was involved. My thought has always been that the ones I saw were some type of plasma energy.

The **MLs we observed would turn off and then back on repeatedly. They also varied in intensity.** Sometimes they just went out and stayed out. **We observed MLs that were stationary and others that would travel left or right.** Sometimes a single ML or a group of MLs would reverse direction. They did not seem to gain or lose much altitude in our observations. I do not recall seeing any that appeared at ground level and then rose to altitude. Our recollection is that they seemed to appear out of nothing, slightly above the horizon or skyline, and then do their amazing antics. We saw both long and short duration events.

Comment:

This is an excellent report from careful observers. Details of their report are consistent with most of my observations with two important exceptions:

1) During the late 60's time frame they report frequent ML appearances in contrast to my 2001 to 2012 observations that were extremely infrequent. If MLs are likely products of tectonic forces, *something the author suggests later in this book*, it is reasonable to expect periods of activity and inactivity.

2) Most of the MLs that Hollis and Linda observed would first appear above the horizon. In contrast, most of the MLs I have observed and recorded were located in the air, but below background mesas. On occasion my automated cameras have captured higher flying MLs. *The issue of what controls altitude above terrain is interesting, and is a topic of discussion later in this book. Readers will also find a later discussion of High Flying MLs.*

SL Story #2 Five MLs hovered nearby
Time: July 1988
Story from Charlotte Allen, as told to J. Bunnell

Charlotte and her husband Richard (now deceased) took a twelve-year-old relative to Mitchell Flat to look for MLs. They drove south on a ranch road and parked about a half mile from US 90 to observe. To their amazement, a flight of five MLs came their way and stopped forward motion near the passenger side of the parked car. The MLs hovered and bobbed while holding position perhaps 20 to 50 feet above ground level. They were clearly visible to their young guest, sitting in the front passenger seat, and to Charlotte who was sitting in the back seat on the right side. Richard was unable to see the lights because the car's roof obstructed his view. The lights were in a line at staggered altitudes as they "bobbed and hovered" in the air for perhaps a minute. Then they seemed to run out of energy and began to extinguish one at a time. **As each light extinguished, individual shafts of light emanated from the center, encasing what**

looked like thousands of dust particles. Each in turn, exhausted of energy, disappeared as they fell toward the ground.

SL Story #3 — Too close encounter
Time: September 1993
Story from Charlotte Allen, as told to J. Bunnell

Charlotte and her husband had purchased a new car during the day. That evening they drove out to look for Marfa Lights accompanied by Charlotte's cousin. They not only saw an ML, but watched it advance directly to their car causing temporary panic because door and window switches in their new car were in unfamiliar locations. The ML stopped suddenly about two feet in front of side windows, almost as if it had been startled by its own reflection. After a brief "inquisitive" hover, the light darted away in the direction it had come from. It was a remarkable and unforgettable encounter.

Comment:
MLs that approach and briefly hover two feet away are not car lights and MLs that lose energy and fall to the ground, are clearly not car lights or mirages. Most ML sightings do not involve close encounters, but those that do are unmistakable encounters. Charlotte Allen is a very credible source.

SL Story #4 — A night I will never forget
Time: July 1969
Email from Linda Shaw

An abundance of atmospheric energy in the mountains surrounding the Marfa Plateau attracts gliding enthusiasts from around the world. In the 60's, national soaring competitions held at Marfa made use of the old Army Airfield next to where the Marfa Lights View Park is now located. In July, 1969, there was not yet a view park, but the abandoned WWII air field was open because of the national soaring event held there. At that time, some hangers were still standing even though the runways had long since become over grown with desert plant life.

After hearing Marfa Light stories, my husband and I, accompanied by my brother, decided to go looking for them. We arrived at the airfield in the late afternoon and drove past the hanger area where hooting owls contributed an eerie sense of mystery. Were we going to get to see these mystery lights and what will they look like? There were no other people anywhere in sight. We elected to drive further south on the abandoned runways, picking our way through desert plant life that had grown up through cracks in the pavement. We continued as far south as the runway system permitted, and then waited for darkness.

Not too long after dark, an amazing light show began. The events we observed that night will remain with us forever. Multiple lights started appearing slowly, and then increased in numbers. Lights would appear and get brighter and then dim and go completely out, only to reappear elsewhere. The **lights were multiple colors and at times there were more than a dozen active.** Then came the best part of the night. **MLs had grouped together and varied in color from reddish to sort of blue green and almost clear.** They became very active with **one or two shooting out to the side to travel long distances and disappear,** never traveling very high.

These more intense periods of activity occurred several times that night, interspersed with periods when they reappeared as just two or three lights in the distance, with little movement. It was almost as if they were recharging or something, but we had no idea. Sometimes they stayed out for several minutes. When the lights appeared closer together, there would be more activity.

After watching for two or three hours, we threaded our way back through the runway weeds and brush to US 90 and drove to Marfa where we stopped at a gas station for fuel. The service station attendant said he had worked at the airfield testing car tires for a company. He said that the location where we had been was very active with Marfa Lights and he had seen them many times there, as had others working at the old airbase. He said one night a fairly large light had glowed close to him. It was larger than most and he could see through it; then it disappeared. That was his story, and he seemed sincere, but it was apparently no big deal to people who lived in the area. **They saw them often back then.**

Comment:

Linda's story reinforces the idea that Marfa Lights were more frequently seen in the 60's than was the case during my investigation (2001 to 2012).

SL Story # 5   Frightened by a Marfa Light

Time: circa 1960's [Note: I have followed Linda Shaw's story with this one because of obvious similarities. The "mechanic" in the two stories may, or may not, be one and the same person.]

This is a second-hand story emailed to J. Bunnell

A good friend related an ML story that involved one of the mechanics, "Karl" (not his real name), who was working at the old Army Airfield as a contractor in support of tire testing activity in the 60's. They had a tire-testing contract there at the time and test vehicles needed to be serviced and tires changed. Karl was working alone in the main hanger at night when the ML event happened. At the time, he was leaning over the engine compartment of a car with his body halfway under the hood when light appeared on the floor below. He did not pay much attention to it because cars were constantly coming and going at all hours. He kept working until **he realized that there had not been any noise** nor did he hear anyone opening and shutting a car door. So he pushed himself out from under the hood for a look. When he turned around, there was no car or truck. Instead there was **a silent super-bright light, as big as a basketball, floating a couple of feet off the ground.** In no way was this normal! The ball of light scared him badly and he reacted by running to his automobile and driving away as fast as possible. Karl was physically unharmed, but the experience was unnerving and he quit not long afterward.

Comment:

The person who related the story remembered the worker's name and the story seems credible. I cannot help but wonder if the filling station attendant in Marfa who talked to Linda Shaw and her husband and her brother in the prior story could have been "Karl?" I have heard a few other similar stories from Alpine and Marfa residents. Stories like this may be why some Marfa/Alpine natives refer to MLs as spook lights.

SL Story #6   An ML bursting high overhead
Time: Winter 2011
Personal account by J. Bunnell

One night after becoming bored waiting for an ML to appear, I was lying on my back watching for satellites to pass overhead. To my surprise, I started seeing bursts of light almost directly overhead. These bursts of light were occurring every few seconds and they looked to be extremely high. They were point bursts of light that did not have light trajectories, as would meteors or aircraft. The displays were more akin to 4th of July fireworks, but they could not have been fireworks because they appeared to be thousands of feet in the air. The kind of altitude I might expect for commercial airliners flying close to 40,000 feet. They just kept happening one at a time in the same small region of sky and I realized that they certainly qualified as mysterious lights (MLs), albeit with different characteristics than anything I had seen before. A View Park visitor and my wife, Sandra, also observed these remarkable high altitude displays. We were witnessing white bursts of light every few seconds located approximately above the nearby old Army Airfield and therefore almost directly overhead. There was no way to reposition my telescope-camera combination to an angle that steep and therefore no way to photograph them. These bursts of white light continued for perhaps ten or fifteen minutes. We watched until these displays ended.

I was shocked to realize that these ML events, located very high in the sky and almost directly overhead, would have gone completely unnoticed if I had not started scanning for satellites. None of my automated night cameras were positioned to photograph high overhead. It made me wonder, how many similar ML events might have been missed? After that experience, I started toting an extra camera capable of being used vertically and tried to remember to glance overhead from time to time. But this wake-up call happened not too long before the end of my investigation, so I cannot say if overhead MLs I observed that night are extremely rare, or not.

The next three people stories were previously published in Appendix A to **Hunting Marfa Lights** (**HML**). They are reproduced here in condensed form because they include valuable details (I have added bold emphasis) with potential to aid understanding of ML Phenomena.

HML Story #7   Undulating plasma balls
Time: Late summer 1996
Email story submitted by Dirk & Sarah Vander Zee.

My wife and I saw them and I had no idea they are as rare as has been reported. Apparently, we were there on a "super-outbreak" night.

Filmed them on my Sony camcorder. Highly doubt they were mirages. Behavior was **best described as "undulating plasma balls" that folded in on each other, then split, blossomed, divided, rejoined, re-split, then dimmed, bloomed again, then blinked off.** Like spherical torches being suddenly snuffed out. It was a totally moonless night. Many repeats [of these cycles], separated sometimes by 10-15 minutes. Viewed them for 2 plus hours, from both the "viewing area" and also down south along Nopal Road. Totally bizarre.

Certainly not the Presidio highway lights which were easily seen off in a different direction. These were of a much different hue, and more importantly, visible through the telescopic view finder, and in a totally black field of view. I could actually lock and focus [the camera] on them on most occasions, while **they were [performing] some sort of internal movement, best described as multi-spectrum light folding in on itself, spherically shaped.**

On return to the ranch house where we were staying that night **we saw several depressed areas in the ground that glowed a soft, ethereal blue light, as if some dim blue gas were poured into these small depressions about the size of a swimming pool, and left to slowly be absorbed into the ground.**

No explanation. Certainly not headlights. No way a mirage, as we were literally within feet of these particular phenomena.
Theory: I don't think they are "gases" although the pools of blue light were stunning. It is some form of electrical or plasma energy "field" that has a surface exit point near Marfa. Or not. Go see for yourself.

Comment:

Dirk provides a clear description of the Marfa Lights phenomenon, some of which are consistent with my own observations. What makes this report special is reference to the pools of blue light existing in round depressions later that night. Also, his observation, **"...some sort of internal movement"** within the lights is interesting. Both are keen observations of important details.

HML Story #10   Getting hooked
Time: November 2000
Personal account: Jim Bunnell and wife Marlene (deceased)

November 25:

In November 2000 my [now deceased] wife Marlene and I traveled to Carlsbad, NM for a Thanksgiving visit. After Thanksgiving we decided to take a side excursion to Marfa to look at the Mystery Lights. I grew up in Marfa/Presidio and knew of the lights but I had not seen them in over 40 years and Marlene had never seen them. We arrived at the primary viewing site at sundown. The WWII Army Airfield where I played as a child was long gone. We parked nearby at the View Park [a much smaller park at that time] and watched gathering darkness for any unusual lights.

With no clouds and no moon on that Saturday night, there was a dark clear sky, ideal for viewing lights. As it became dark we could see fixed red lights (both flashing and steady) and fixed green lights. These lights were constant in their behavior and were clearly not mysterious. We could also observe distant car lights that would pop in and out of view to the southwest. These automobile lights were not difficult to distinguish because they followed repeating patterns of motion and moved only to the right [north] as they traveled Highway 67 on their way from Presidio to Marfa.

Soon after dark we saw two strange lights on a compass bearing almost due south from our viewing location. These lights pulsed independently and seemed to follow a random sequence that, in most cases, went from dark to relatively dim, flared to a higher level of brightness, then dimmed and eventually became dark again.

Sometimes both lights would be on at the same time. The **lights were orange-white although the one on the left did turn orange-red**

once or twice. Altitude of the lights could not be determined but both were well below the horizon. The one on the right was somewhat lower than the other and **frequently would dim so much as to become invisible to the naked eye even though it could still be detected through seven-power binoculars as a glow on surrounding brush.** The lights may have had minor horizontal and/ or vertical movement, but that could not be determined with our limited equipment. Sometimes they did appear to descend behind obstructing brush such that only an indirect glow could be seen. This appearance of vertical motion was more frequently observed with the lower light (the one on the right).

We were not alone at the viewing site. A number of other vehicles came, left, or stayed and people milled about and commented on the same lights we were observing. I took another bearing on these same lights from one mile east of the primary site to accomplish triangulation. We continued to view these two lights for about two and one-half hours and then returned to our motel in Alpine. I returned to the site at about 1:00 AM that same night and resumed observation of these two lights until they extinguished at 2:30 AM. Although I remained at the viewing site until approximately 4:00 AM, they did not reappear.

From my youth, I knew Marfa's Mystery Lights were truly mysterious but these seemed too perfect. **Wind was north at 16 mph with significant gusts, but no wind response was observed in these stationary lights,** suggesting to me, at the time, that they might be electric lights attached to a frame. Both Marlene and I could not help but wonder if Marfa citizens had arranged some sort of light display to encourage tourism. The lights we observed that Saturday night were few in number, appeared to be located not too far from the viewing site, came on promptly after dark, went off completely at 2:30 AM., and exhibited only small movements, if any. This pattern was too consistent and seemed a little too pat. Were these lights being artificially produced to attract viewers?

Unknown to us, Sharon Eby Cornet and family members were also viewing these same lights on November 25th from a much closer vantage point on Nopal Road as reported in ***Hunting Marfa Lights***, Story 9, page 212. Sharon reported that the lights were holding their positions while illuminating brush and terrain below them, as I also observed from the View Park, eliminating any possibility that we were observing mirages.

November 26

Sunday night I returned alone to the viewing site determined to find out if these strange displays were maybe not so strange after all. I arrived shortly after dark and found the viewing area once again covered up with other visitors already intently watching the night's light displays. Mysterious lights were again visible from the same location and continued to play their "now you see me, now you don't" pattern I had observed the night before. To my astonishment, on this second evening they were accompanied by numerous other lights located to the left and the right of the original location. In total, there may have been as many as eleven lights with as many as eight emitting simultaneously.

This array of lights ranged from about 168 to 258 degrees magnetic from my location at the View Park. In the spot occupied the previous night by the single right-hand light, there were now two, and sometimes as many as three, bright lights arranged in a closely spaced horizontal row. The total number of lights observed on this second night, and their wide distribution, cast considerable doubt on my suspicion that they might be artificially generated.

I was very tempted to walk to these lights, but recognized such an attempt would be foolish given the dark night and the certainty that lying between my location and the target area were many cacti, barbed wire, and possibly snakes, not to mention cow patties. It was unpleasant to even think about walking into a cactus wearing Nike running shoes. Also my clothing was not adequate to withstand the Marfa night air with temperatures in the low 30's and made colder by wind. Moreover, I had no permission to enter ranch properties (trespassing is illegal in Texas!).

Comment:

It was these two nights of observations that so intrigued my interest. I searched books, libraries, the internet and the local University to find information that might explain what I had observed. There were lots of theories, but none of them worked; they were all flawed. In the pursuit of real answers, I ended up doing my own privately funded investigation that lasted much longer than I had anticipated (12 years). This book summarizes the results of that long-term study.

HML Story #13   No wind response
Time: March 30/31, 2002
Personal account by author

I traveled to Marfa in March, 2002, not to look for Mystery Lights, but to see the new View Park expansion and to obtain daylight range data of known objects in Mitchell Flat using a Swiss Army range finder. After my trip of 500 miles, I arrived at the View Park at 11:30 PM, saw the freshly opened facility and talked to a few park visitors, but I saw nothing unusual. The following day I used the range finder in daylight to more accurately locate regular light sources and various structures in Mitchell Flat. That night I observed a single fairly dim light about one-half hour after dark. Given its dim glow and direction, I suspected it was most likely an automobile on Nopal Road. This light stayed on continuously and, on a few occasions, briefly flared to high brightness. I continued to suspect this was only an automobile light. Then a second light appeared left of the first light, the two lights started flashing together brightly and then merged into one light followed by separation again into two lights. In response, I began observing these lights carefully. The second (left) light went out but the original light continued to burn dimly and to occasionally flash to high brightness. The second light made a few more appearances, but the merge event was not repeated. The original light continued to emit dim light with occasional flashes to brightness for at least two more hours. During this time I observed with 20 power tripod-mounted binoculars. **These above-ground lights remained anchored in the same location even though a noticeable wind was blowing.** Wind velocities were later determined to have been 8-12 miles per hour with occasional gusts to 22 m.p.h. I was impressed by the fact that these **MLs never showed any reaction or response to the wind; they remained rock steady without any wind response even though they were clearly above the ground and the wind was gusty.**

Unlike the left light, the one on the right never went out completely during the two to three-hour event. The Swiss range finder could not be used in the dark and, without range information or a compass, I was unable to determine where the lights were located. Based on their unusual behavior, I became convinced that these lights were definitely not automobile lights. Times between flashes to brightness were of relatively long duration, much too long for the patience of someone wishing to hoax.

Comment:

This sighting was perhaps the third time that I had noticed that multiple stationary MLs tended to string east to west with the more easterly position demonstrating less persistence and sometimes less intensity than the more westerly position. It also served to reinforce the observation that **splitting of the lights always seems to occur during a bright phase while merging might occur during a dim phase**. Most important of all, this sighting was a clear demonstration of **MLs holding their positions in strong winds -- not only holding station, but doing so with no bobbing or other evidence of wind influence.** The November 2000 MLs (HML Story #10) had also been stationary in strong winds with no observed wind response. These observations raised important questions. How can anything flying in air not be subject to wind influence? Should be impossible! That would be like a boat holding position in a flowing river without an anchor, engine power, a rope tether, or anything else. This is no small thing. It is a very odd ML property with no obvious explanation.

This sighting was also a reminder that it is difficult to validate potential ML lights of short duration when time is not sufficient to establish strangeness. Had this sighting been of shorter duration, I would likely have written it off as a probable automobile.

In summary, the preceding stories show great diversity; they are not what would be expected if they result only from headlights on Highway 67. Also, the direction of observations, when reported, are to the south or southeast from the View Park (not to the southwest where Highway 67 traffic can be seen).

Even though these ML stories have diversity, they also yield common elements. Observers reported that MLs:

1. Turn On/Off repeatedly.
2. Vary in brightness.
3. Divide, merge, and eject particles.
4. Split (usually in conjunction with increased brightness).
5. Most commonly appear as white, yellow and/or yellow-orange (but other colors are seen on occasion).
6. Move horizontally more than vertically, especially for MLs illuminating close to the ground.
7. Show more stability in a center point (given multiple lights).
8. Display internal flames and movements.
9. Can hold stationary or travel cross country.
10. Illuminate brush and terrain below their location when flying close to the ground (something Mirages are unable to do).
11. Sometimes lose energy and extinguish as they fall.
12. Are silent!
13. Show no wind response! [This characteristic has no easy explanation and is addressed, in more detail, in later chapters].

Chapter 2
WHERE Are Those Lights?

Figure 6. First-time visitors often have no idea which way to look for MLs and frequently end up focusing on headlights of cars to the southwest. Vehicle lights appear nightly on US 67 and are visible even before dark.

Where to Look

Map 2 shows the location of the Marfa Lights View Park in relation to Marfa, Alpine, and most importantly, Mitchell Flat. The View Park is on US 90, nine miles east of Marfa. New visitors to the Marfa Lights View Park find themselves on a nice concrete platform conveniently equipped with public binoculars (it is best to take your own when you visit) but are given no information regarding which way to look for MLs. This main "Viewing Platform" is oriented facing southwest (207.7 degrees true or 200.4 degrees magnetic) and provides good views to the east, south, and west.

The difference between "true" and "magnetic" directional bearings is known as "declination." It is the difference between the geographical meridian (true north) and magnetic north. Declination varies by geographic location and can also vary over time. In Mitchell Flat, declination is 7.3 degrees (magnetic angles = true angles - 7.3 degrees). In this book most directions are shown as magnetic angles because they are compass bearings (Exception: **Maps 1 & 2** have true bearing indicators while **Maps 3 - 10** have arrows indicating both True North and Magnetic North). If you are using a GPS app to measure angles, it may provide true angles or may give you a choice of magnetic or true.

In this chapter I use magnetic angles to help readers identify which direction they are looking, but you may think of these as simply convenient labels. You will not need a compass to keep track of which way to look provided you arrive at the View Park before dark and have time to become oriented. If you do elect to use a compass, keep in mind that the View Park pavilion has steel rebar in the concrete floor, steel railings, steel

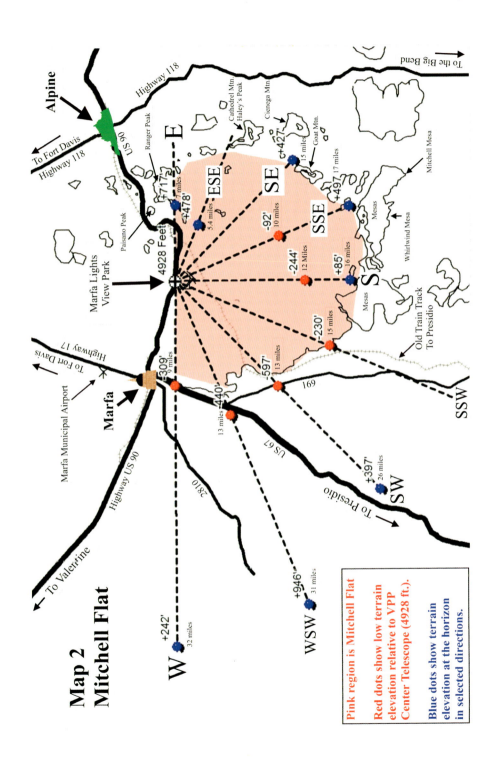

Figure 7. A telephone microwave tower near Highway 169 is located 12.5 statute miles southwest of the View Park. This view was photographed from Highway 169. Car lights on Highway 67 are visible nightly southwest from the View Park. This tower flashes white during the day and red after dark (see **Figure 8**).

columns plus steel overhead and all that steel has potential to degrade compass accuracy. All of my compass readings were taken on the grounds to the south of the Pavilion, usually near the western-most plaque (see **Map 1**). I have called this the SW Plaque in this book.

Now allow me to lay out what you will see as you look in directions available from the View Park Pavilion.

Southwest : Vehicle lights are clearly visible nightly in this direction.

Soon after dark, new visitors begin seeing, to the southwest, unexplained lights that seem to appear out of nowhere and are moving left to right. It is easy to see why first-time visitors are likely to assume that those bright lights are the very Marfa Lights they hoped to see. Instead they are watching headlights from traffic descending a mountain road

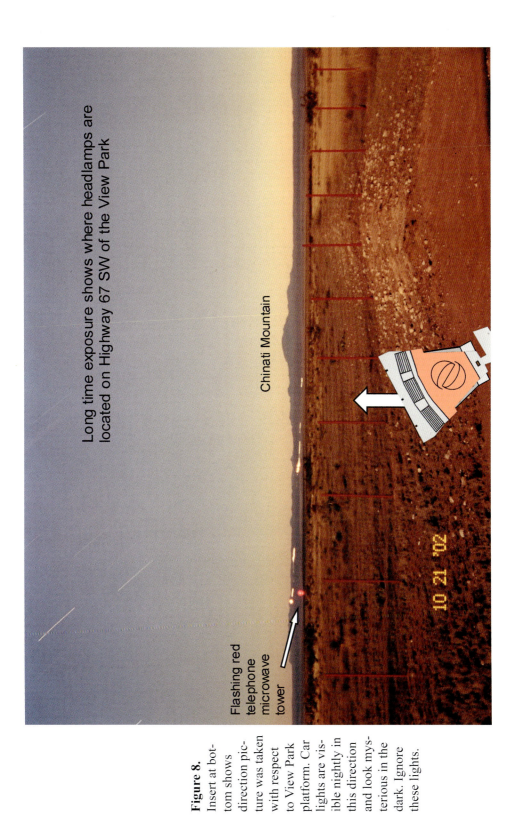

Figure 8. Insert at bottom shows direction picture was taken with respect to View Park platform. Car lights are visible nightly in this direction and look mysterious in the dark. Ignore these lights.

Flashing red telephone microwave tower

Chinati Mountain

Long time exposure shows where headlamps are located on Highway 67 SW of the View Park

(Highway 67) on their way from Presidio to Marfa. These lights are so far away (16 to 25 miles) that taillights of southbound traffic are not visible. The headlights at that range are clearly visible, but merged into one bright light for each vehicle. The fact that they are traveling a winding mountain road causes perceived intensity of these headlights to vary as a function of how well road segments align with the View Park. Periodically masked by terrain, the lights "appear" and "disappear," mimicking ML behavior. Curving road segments can cause lights in a line of several cars to look as if they are merging or multiplying as they move together or apart as seen from the View Park. If that is not enough to confuse the issue, darkness hides the mountains and makes it seem like the lights are moving through the air above terrain instead of driving on it. These nightly headlights to the southwest are a great source of confusion for first-time visitors and a bonanza for skeptics and pseudo-scientists.

You will want to ignore these car lights and look elsewhere. Fortunately, there is an easy way to do that thanks to a telephone microwave tower to the southwest that is tall enough to be equipped with a red, flashing light to alert low-flying aircraft. This tower, located 12.5 miles from the View Park, displays, in daylight, a flashing white light that changes to red after dark, making it easy to see (**Figures 7 & 8**). Vehicle lights first come into view to the left of and above this flashing red light as they top the roadway's summit. Continuing to the right, they move past and above the red tower light and continue descending toward Marfa, losing altitude as the roadway descends.

Figure 8 is a four-hour time exposure that turns night into day and reveals where headlights on Highway 67 are visible with respect to the flashing red tower and Chinati Mountain. The small inset drawing at the bottom of **Figure 8** represents the park's "Viewing Platform" with an arrow indicating the direction that the picture was taken from, with respect to the platform orientation. This approximate "picture orientation" representation is also used on other landscape pictures

Figure 9. Looking West from View Park Platform just after sunset. Marfa is in this direction.

West :   A possible direction to look, but not the best.

The view west includes light sources located south and west of Marfa (**Figure 9**). Edson Hendricks (author of the 1991 "*A Three Ring Circus*" story in ***Hunting Marfa Lights***) and Fred Tenny have witnessed MLs to the west and they are both careful observers, so there are legitimate reasons to look west for MLs. Light sources I have photographed west of the View Park, when analyzed, have all turned out to be vehicle lights on Highway 2810, or other roads to the west. Bottom line: You may find MLs west of the View Park, but your chances are better looking southeast or south (less chance of confusion with vehicle lights).

North: Not a favorable direction to look.

When I was 9 or 10 years old and living in Marfa, I remember people getting excited by UFOs seen northwest of town on at least two consecutive nights. Today I suspect that what caused all of that excite-

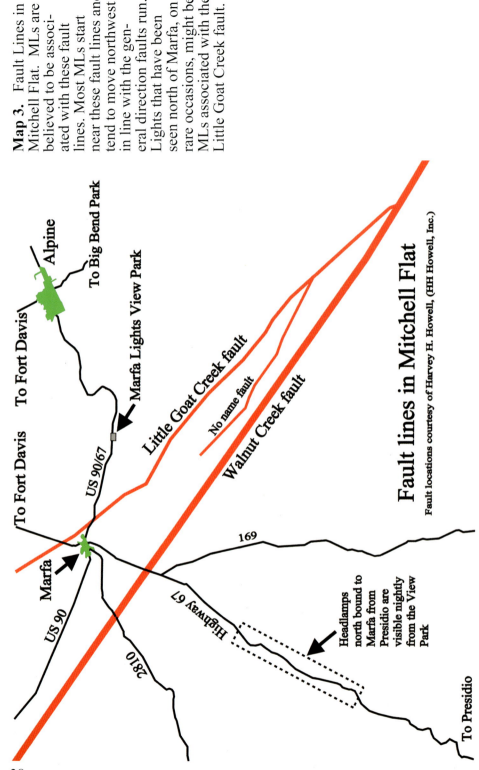

Map 3. Fault Lines in Mitchell Flat. MLs are believed to be associated with these fault lines. Most MLs start near these fault lines and tend to move northwest in line with the general direction faults run. Lights that have been seen north of Marfa, on rare occasions, might be MLs associated with the Little Goat Creek fault.

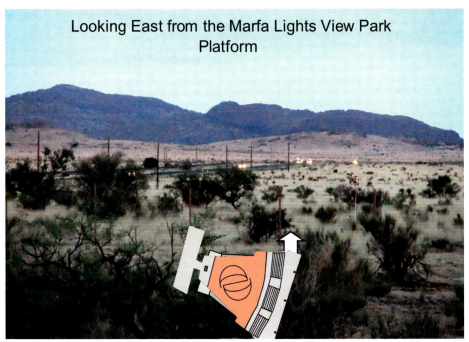

Figure 10. Looking east from View Park platform includes traffic on US 90 as well as train traffic.

Figure 11. Beautiful Cathedral Mountain as seen from the View Park platform looking east.

ment were MLs somewhere north of Marfa along the Little Goat Creek fault line (**Map 3**). If so, they actually were MLs -- not alien craft. People have reported seeing MLs north of US 90, but the View Park platform does not accommodate views to the north and the odds of seeing anything interesting are likely to be severely diminished as compared to looking south and southeast.

East: Not a great direction to look either (Figure 10 and 11).

The View Park platform does accommodate observation to the East and, from time to time, people have reported seeing MLs in that direction, but I have to rate it as "not the best direction to look." As you will notice on the location maps provided in the "Best Evidence" chapter, there is a nighttime dirt road that provides access from US 90 to the 101 ranch complex. Vehicles are frequently observed on this road, especially early in the evening. They will usually be moving either north or south, in line with the road directions, often close enough to the View Park that headlight beams and/or taillights can be observed with good binoculars.

Lights seen in this direction could certainly be MLs, but more often than not, they will be vehicle lights. Look to see if they travel south to the 101 ranch complex or north to US 90.

Southeast and South: These are good directions to look for MLs.

In my experience, some of the best MLs have made their first appearance southeast or south of the View Park, to the right of Goat Mountain, with mesas in the background. **Figure 12** provides reference directional information from the View Park. Mesa irregularities in this direction are helpful for estimating ML directions from the View Park.

Background mesas located south-southeast (**Figure 13**) and south (**Figure 14**) are smoother with fewer unique terrain features, but these are also good directions to look for MLs, second only to looking southeast.

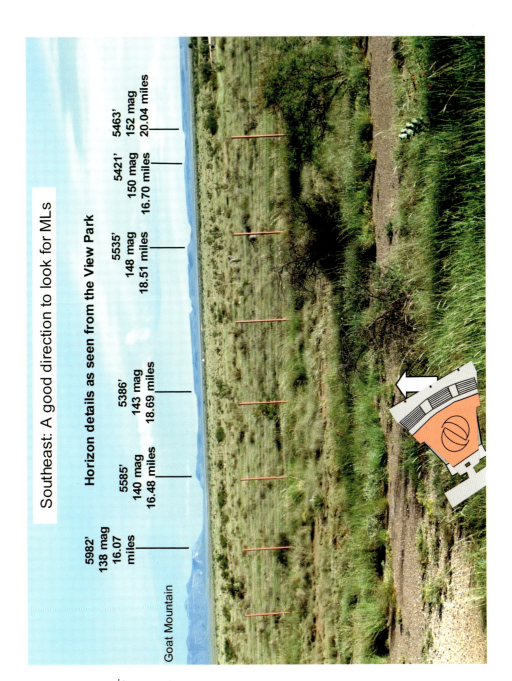

Figure 12. Background mesas located southeast of the Marfa Lights View Park have an irregular horizon profile that is useful for estimating magnetic bearings and elevations of observed MLs. Height of the View Park platform center telescope is 4928 feet above sea level.
True bearings = Magnetic + 7.3 degrees.

Figure 13.
Looking SSE from the Marfa Lights View Park

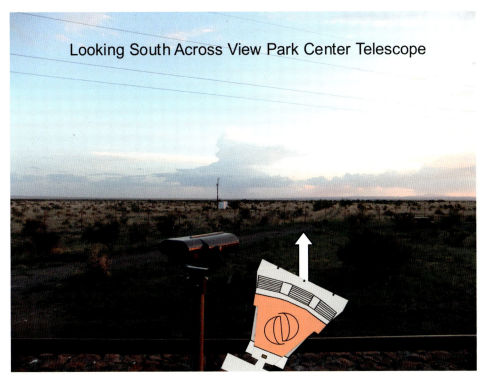

Figure 14. View looking due south over the View Park Center Telescope. The small white house is probably for pumping water. Background mesas are low in this direction. Narrow, curving pavement is left over from the WWII Army Airfield.

Look Up: Some MLs go high into the night sky, as evidenced by the following ML accounts

There is one more important direction to look and that is up. My best color pictures all show MLs flying below background mesas, but Hollis and Linda Fuchs, in their story (SL Story #1, *MLs are not always rare!*) said, "The majority of MLs I saw were high fliers, anywhere from 1 to 5 degrees above the skyline."

They are not alone in reporting MLs flying at higher levels. On January 31, 2002, Bill, along with his wife and granddaughter, reported observing an ML for 10 or 15 minutes that was about 15 degrees above the skyline (HML Story #12). "It would climb in a scooping motion, and then come down as if it were rolling down stairs. It moved very suddenly from left to right and then back again, all the while becoming brighter and dimmer and changing colors from yellow-white to red. Vertical movements were estimated to be 10 to 15 degrees and horizontal movements were on the order of 20 to 25 degrees in a back-and-forth motion." The light was still visible when they left the View Park and other people were watching it.

On October 30, 2002, I and others on the View Park platform observed an orange light in the sky, moving left to right (HML Story #14). It appeared out of nothing, did not strobe or blink, and disappeared after traveling ten or fifteen degrees with respect to our observation point. It was moving too slowly to be a meteor and did not appear to be an aircraft even though it was definitely an orange ball in the sky.

In late summer of 2003, Dan and his wife witnessed an incredible display of tennis-ball sized fiery red orbs that bounced in the sky, zoomed together, split apart and did all sorts of crazy things (HML Story #20). "At times there would be 6-7 of them bouncing around. They would start from fairly far apart, merge into one, split apart again, and then race off in any number of directions. It was around one AM and we were the only ones in the Marfa Lights View Park. The light display continued for about 30 minutes and then abruptly stopped."

James Nixon III reported seeing a colorful curtain of light extending from just above the horizon to perhaps 12,000 feet that was multicolored, predominantly greenish to rose hues, to violet (HML Story #25). It appeared during, or right after, twilight and shimmered for approximately 30 minutes in the gathering darkness.

Comments

All of the above events were in the sky, but low enough to be noticed by anyone looking in the right direction. When watching for MLs, I used telescopes as camera lenses mounted on tripods designed for field observations. The mounting hardware permitted tilting these scope/

camera combinations sufficiently to have easily captured any of the MLs described above even though the mounting hardware was not intended for astronomical use and could not be safely tilted to angles near vertical. I never considered that a significant limitation until one night in 2011 when a View Park visitor, Sandy, and I watched MLs bursting high overhead for a matter of minutes (see SL Story #6 in Chapter 1).

Chapter 3
Visit the View Park!

Figure 15. A Thursday night scene at the View Park. Weekends tend to be a little more crowded.

Preparations

- **Binoculars:** The View Park has three free stationary binoculars for public use (**Figure 16a**), but it is recommended that you bring your own. Any binoculars will give you better vision than bare eyeballs, but the fact that you will be looking for MLs in the dark favors binoculars with larger objective lenses because they collect more light. A secondary consideration is power. In general, it is better to avoid high power in any optical aid that is going to be hand held (a tripod, however, makes it possible to use higher power lenses effectively).

Figure 16a. View Park Stationary binoculars for public use.

Here is how to select. Binoculars are identified with two numbers, for example, "10 x 50." The first number is the optical power of the lens. A 10 x 50 magnifies the view by 10 times. Objects appear 10 times larger than they do without the binoculars. For hand held use, power in the range of 7 to 10 is probably best. If you are accustomed to holding binoculars, 12 is okay, but you will probably not see much, if any, improvement over ten power. Forget binoculars with zoom control and binoculars with anything greater than 12 power unless you plan to use them with a tripod.

The second number (50 in the above example) is the size of the large lenses (not the eyepieces) in millimeters. Fifty millimeter large lenses ("objectives") are approximately two inches in diameter. The size of the objective lenses determines the light-gathering power of the binoculars. Looking for MLs is a nighttime pursuit so, the larger the lenses, the more you'll see. But as lens size increases, the physical size and weight of the binocular increases. Binoculars with objective lenses larger than 50 are going to be heavier and more tiring to hold.

In general, you can expect 7 x 50 binoculars to be better than 10 x 42 for nighttime use because light collection power of the 50 mm lens outweighs the power advantage of the smaller binoculars.

Binoculars can be very helpful for sorting ranch lights and vehicle lights from MLs. If you do not already own binoculars, consider purchasing 7 X 50, 8 X 50, or 10 x 50 binoculars.

- **Telescopes:** Some visitors have telescopes and like to bring them to the View Park. Optical power of a telescope can be very helpful for detecting light beams and taillights of vehicles in Mitchell Flat. Keep in mind that telescopes have very small fields of view. My experience has been that electronic sights work well for finding low altitude lights that may be many miles away. If your telescope is not already equipped with an electronic sight, you might want to consider adding one (**Figure 16b**).

Figure 16b. My Vixen Optics VMC200L reflector telescope equipped with an electronic sight. Set up near the east end of the View Park platform, waiting for darkness, with Chinati Mountain in the background.

- **Cameras:** If photography is your purpose, then use a tripod (hand held cameras are great for producing interesting squiggly lines that mean absolutely nothing) and a remote shutter release. The camera of choice needs to have enough control to permit selection of exposure time or else be a camera that is capable of selecting correct exposure on its own. If you manually select exposure time, I suggest three- to five-second times. Most exposures that long will work out okay, but it does mean that traveling MLs are going to appear as light tracks, not stationary points of light.

Flash bulbs are useless for targets that are miles away (frequently 20 miles or more in the case of car lights); they serve only to rob people on the view platform of valuable night vision. Please do not join this crowd for they know not what they do.

- **Chairs:** A folding chair of some type may be something you will be glad you brought to the View Park. Hunting for Marfa Lights is a little like going fishing in a lake with few fish. The activity is best termed

"Watchful Waiting." Fear not. Marfa skies are without light pollution and beautiful. You will enjoy the experience whether you are lucky enough to see an ML or not.

- **Clothing:** Expect colder temperature than your daytime experience. The View Park is more than 4900 feet above sea level and the wind blows. My data shows that, on average, atmospheric temperatures were 18 degrees cooler at ML start times than corresponding daytime temperature highs. The combination of lower temperature plus wind may cause you to be uncomfortable, if you are caught unprepared.

Chapter 4

The Art of Rejecting Ordinary Lights

Don't Be Fooled by Ranch Lights

This may seem like a silly admonishment. After all, ranch lights are stationary so there is no reason to be confused about a ranch light, right? Well, surprisingly enough, on multiple occasions I have seen View Park visitors gazing intently at ranch lights, absolutely convinced that the lights are in motion and doing amazing things. Are these crazy people? Not at all. Stare several seconds at a fixed light in a dark background and the light will appear to be moving. This solitary light, minus other visual clues, plays on the functioning of our retinas, sending an illusory message to our brains. It's important to know about this illusion, whether you are a pilot flying at night by following a lead plane's lights, or an observer staring into the night looking for MLs and seeing, instead, ranch lights.

Fortunately, there is an easy way to identify fixed lights. There are a number of vertical poles on the View Park platform as well as power poles and fence posts in view. Pick a convenient fixed pole and line it up with the light you are observing. The motion of the ranch light will immediately stop and stay stopped.

Ranch lights can be helpful to knowing which direction you are looking in the dark. Ranch house light locations are also useful when it comes to spotting vehicle lights in Mitchell Flat. In general, any light that starts at a ranch complex or goes to a ranch complex is likely to be a vehicle light. **Map 4** provides reference locations of selected ranch complexes that are sometimes visible from the View Park viewing platform.

Eliminating Vehicle Lights

Presidio to Marfa Highway Lights

Ignore headlights southwest of the View Park on Highway 67. Car lights on this Presidio to Marfa mountain highway do look mysterious to the uninitiated. Fortunately, they are the easiest false targets to recognize and eliminate. Be sure to review **Figure 8** because it shows exactly where

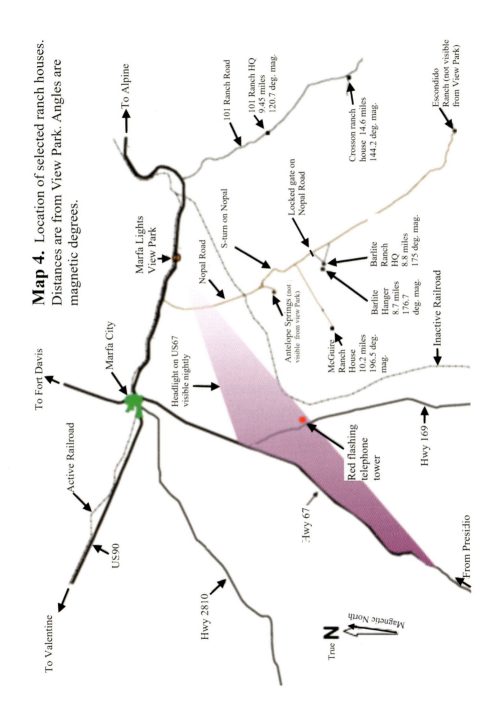

Map 4. Location of selected ranch houses. Distances are from View Park. Angles are magnetic degrees.

those headlights are located with respect to the red flashing telephone tower that is located near Highway 169 (**Figure 7**). Do MLs ever appear in that direction? Yes, it does happen, but rarely. I never look in that direction unless I have been following an ML that began life further east and moved far enough west to reach or pass the red flashing telephone tower.

It is important to understand where those Highway 67 car lights appear! Not looking in that direction will put you ahead of the game compared to most casual View Park visitors.

Watch for Light Beams

A bigger challenge is eliminating vehicle lights in Mitchell Flat. Six of the maps provided in this book show the location of what I call nighttime roads in Mitchell flat. These are the main feeder dirt roads. They consist of the 101 Ranch road system at the east end of Mitchell Flat, and Nopal Road, which takes a diagonal route right through the middle of Mitchell Flat. I call these "nighttime roads" because they are likely to have at least some traffic every night as ranch people drive into town, return from town, or go to visit another ranch complex.

This is where the binoculars and/or telescope that you thoughtfully brought along can help because you may be able to spot light beams created by headlights. **MLs do not have light beams; they emit light in all directions. In contrast, just about all artificial lights have reflectors to send the light in a directional beam.** While you are looking for light beams, also look for red tail lights following closely.

When Vehicles Are Too Far Away to See Their Light Beams

But what if you did not bring optical aids or else the ones you have are unable to provide that level of detail because the lights you are observing are too distant? What other clues might Sherlock Homes fall back on to identify vehicle lights? Remember the following general rules of observation because they can be helpful, particularly if you are inexperienced in looking for MLs.

1. Unknown lights east of the View Park. If the unknown light is located east of the View Park and is moving either north or south, then it is may be a vehicle driving on the 101 Ranch road system. When I see unknown lights at the east end of Mitchell Flat that are moving north or south, I automatically suspect they are VLs (vehicle lights), and they stay in that category unless, and until, they exhibit behavior that is unmistakably characteristic of MLs (e.g., they turn On/Off repeatedly, or vary greatly in brightness, or fly above terrain, or perform splits and merges, or explode).

2. Unknown lights south of the View Park, moving east or southeast. If lights are traveling east or southeast there is a good chance they may be vehicles unless they exhibit ML-like behaviors (e.g., turning On/Off, splitting merging, orbiting, or expanding and contracting). MLs sometimes do travel east or southeast (or any direction) for a time, but their most common direction of travel is to the northwest. That makes lights moving east or southeast at least suspect. Look for headlight beams and/or red taillights versus ML characteristics.

3. Unknown lights south of the View Park, moving west or northwest. There are two important filters for eliminating vehicles traveling northwest on Nopal Road. The first is the locked gate located about half a mile east of Barlite Ranch, as seen from the View Park. This locked gate was a huge benefit to my investigation because, during that time frame, the gate was entirely manual. Vehicles would stop and someone would walk to the gate to open a combination padlock, push open the gate, and get back into the vehicle to drive through. Then the gate had to be re-locked before proceeding on. This resulted in a significant stop in a known location. Any lights that paused at the gate radial (i.e. direction from the camera) were clearly vehicle lights and those that passed the gate radial without stopping, were likely to be MLs.

Today the rules are a bit different because the locked gate can be opened remotely from vehicles. But this vital stop point has not gone away completely. It may still be usable as a vehicle filter, but the time delay of gate passage is now a good deal shorter. Nevertheless, it is still detectable in most cases because the automatic gate opens a little slowly. Of course, some ranchers and ranch hands start opening the gate before they get there and are able to pass through quickly. I do not know if they can do that without stopping, but it is possible they can.

There is another sure way to detect vehicles driving northwest on Nopal Road. Conveniently, Nopal Road has an S-turn located almost due south (179 degrees magnetic; aka 186 degrees true) that sends their head-lights directly across the View Park (**Map 5**). This S-turn in the roadway results in a very bright flash of head-lights that is unobstructed, unmistakable, and will not be missed if you are ready for it.

Finding the Locked Gate and Nopal Road S-turn Locations

How can you be ready to detect either one of these vehicle detection filter points? The answer is that you just need to know where to look and be ready for the potential pause at the locked gate and for the headlight flash at the Nopal S-turn. To properly prepare, you need to be at the View Park at or before sunset so that you can get oriented to locations while there is adequate daylight. Imagine that you are at the View Park as the sun is setting, or has just set. Look south (left of the small white pump house easily visible beyond the fence line, but still close to the View Park; review **Map 1**) and find a big square building in the distance (8.7 miles). That big building is the Barlite Ranch hanger and it is located at `~177 degrees magnetic (**Figure 17**). You do not need to worry about knowing that angle.

Look left of the hanger building and, before dark, you will be able to see the Barlite ranch complex. With binoculars it is pretty easy to locate and even easier after dark because the ranch has a sodium vapor light on a pole. Angular separation between center of the Barlite ranch complex and their hanger, as seen from the View Park, is about 2 degrees. So this

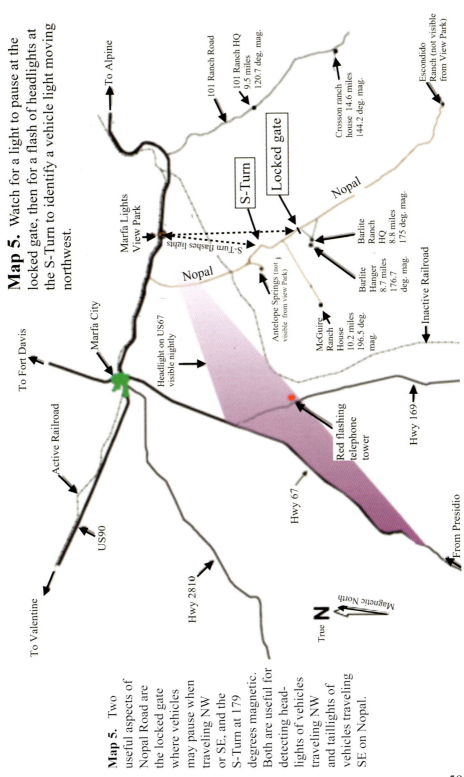

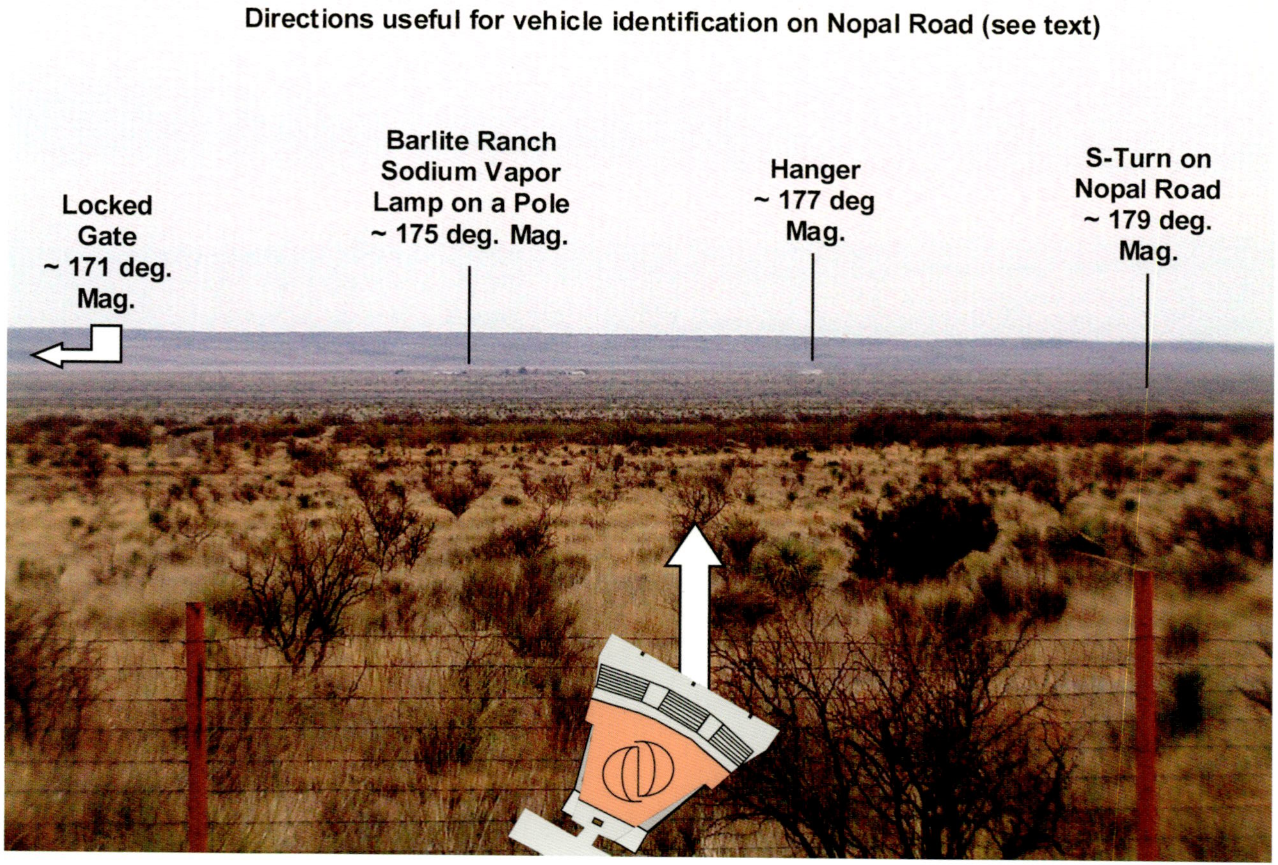

Figure 17. The locked gate on Nopal Road at 171 degrees magnetic from the View Park and the S-Curve, also on Nopal Road at 179 degrees magnetic, provide useful points of observation for detection of vehicle traffic on Nopal road.

preparation procedure is simple. The locked gate is twice that angle to the left of Barlite HQ and the S-turn is twice that angle right of Barlite HQ. In daylight, locate these two critical directions (you only have to know their locations approximately) and select some View Park or fence line detail that can be used to identify those approximate directions while you still have daylight.

By the way, you can also use the S-curve to look for taillights if you are tracking a light that is moving east or southeast.

[Note] Vehicles traveling with speed on dirt roads (they are all dirt in Mitchell Flat) kick up dust that is visible in daylight, twilight, and with good moon light. MLs do not kick up dust and do not have reflector directed light beams.

Ranch Trails

Mitchell Flat is ranch country. It is divided into pastures by barbwire and/or electric fences. Bulls sometimes decide to go right though those fences for whatever reason. Cattle also knock down fences by trying to scratch their backs on the fence posts. And then there are the effects of wind, erosion, and wear and tear. Part of the ranching task is to patrol those fences and repair any damaged sections. In the past, ranchers rode the fences on horseback, but today they use trucks. These trucks are big, 3/4 or one ton vehicles equipped with four-wheel drive and plenty of ground clearance. They can go most anywhere. As a result, fence lines usually have well-worn truck tracks on one or both sides of the fence. Those trucks also get driven off-road to other points of interest such as water tanks, feeding troughs, and blocks of salt. In short, there exists an elaborate complex of truck trails all over Mitchell Flat. These "trails" are rough in spots with sand traps year around and mud holes during the rainy season. These ranch trails are frequently used during daylight hours and are distinct enough to be seen with aerial or satellite photography so they can be found on some detailed maps of the region. Maps that include them make it look like there are roads everywhere in Mitchell Flat.

The germane question is, are they ever used by anyone at night when MLs are being seen and, if they are, how can anyone know that this extensive system of ranch trails is not the real source of the uncommon lights I call MLs? That is a fair question to ask. By 2008, I was using up to ten automated cameras nightly. Those terabytes of video were indeed time-consuming to review, but they afforded unusual insight into details necessary to filter out occasional lights made by vehicles driving ranch trails after dark. Fortunately, such activity is indeed rare.

Headlights from these ranch trails after dark do differ from MLs in two important ways. Stationary truck lights are nothing more than stationary lights. Stationary MLs, on the other hand, are variable energy displays, distinctly different than headlamps of a parked vehicle. Vehicles driving ranch trails move slowly (10 to 20 mph is about the limit), especially at night when headlight beams are moving up and down because of rough terrain. MLs, in contrast, are likely to travel cross-country at much higher speeds, on the order of 50 to 100 mph and sometimes much faster. The only time truck and automobile speeds get fast enough to be possible MLs is when they are traveling Nopal or the 101 Ranch roads. That is when the locked gate and S-Turn on Nopal play such important roles. With a light moving northwest, watch for a pause at the locked gate and watch for head lights to flash brightly as the vehicle negotiates the S-Turn. If there is no pause at the gate and you do not see a bright flash at the S-Turn, and the lights are moving too fast to be a vehicle driving on ranch trails, then you can be confident that you are indeed watching an ML. With a light moving southeast, watch for taillights.

All of this may sound a little complicated, but the methodology is actually simple and doable. You just need to do your pre-dark preparation of knowing where to look for important markers (e.g., the S-Turn and the locked gate) and then remember to do so.

Chapter 5
FAQs
(Frequently Asked Questions)

When do MLs appear?

1. Do these lights show up nightly?
A: During my investigation, MLs appearances have been rare. Infrequency and unpredictability of appearance have been the biggest obstacles to learning more about them.

2. Is there a month or season that has more, or better, opportunities?
A: Data I have collected suggest that there is no better month or season of the year.

3. Are MLs more likely to appear in cold weather or hot weather?
A: I have seen them on extremely cold nights as well as very warm nights.

4. Are MLs more likely to appear on stormy nights or clear nights?
A: While on site, I have seen them more often on stormy nights. Automated camera video reviews suggest that weather is probably not a factor in their appearance.

5. Is there a time that would be better to try to see the ML's? Or any time after dark?
A: MLs can appear any time of the night, but no earlier than 30 minutes after sunset. They are more likely during the first 4 hours after sunset.

Where is the best place to watch for MLs?

6. Are the lights visible from any other areas besides the official viewing platform?
A: Yes, they are, but I highly recommend watching from the View Park

for two reasons. First, I have watched for MLs from many different locations and have to say that the Marfa Lights View Park is a nearly perfect location for that purpose. Second, almost all of Mitchell Flat is private land and trespassing on private property is illegal in Texas (I have always been careful to obtain permission before entering private ranch land).

7. Has anyone set-up cameras closer to where the lights appear to be"
A: Between 2006 and 2011, I operated nine to ten automated cameras stationed at four different locations in Mitchell Flat (Roofus, Snoopy, Owlbert A and Owlbert B). These cameras ran every night and I have personally reviewed all of the terabytes of video they collected.

8. Has anyone ever investigated the location where these lights originate?
A: Based on triangulation using multiple (as many as ten) recording video cameras, I have calculated ML locations many times and readers will find a few computed ML locations in Chapter 6 *"**Best Evidence**"* (see Appendix for discussion of positional uncertainties). Based on data collected, it is safe to conclude that MLs rarely have a common point of origin. In some locations (with ranch owner approval), it has been possible to search out areas where MLs might have originated (uncertainty ellipses). Nothing unusual has ever been found on the surface that might explain the source of MLs. I believe that their real points of origins are deep underground as discussed in Chapter 7, *"What Are Those Lights?"*

Has anyone ever attempted to collect ML spectra?

9. Has anyone ever tried to do a spectral analysis to determine the elements emitting the lights?
A: There have been many efforts by multiple people to obtain spectra of Earth Lights of the type seen near Marfa. Dr. Massimo Teodorani, an Italian scientist, is an expert in this field and has written many scientific

papers on Earth Lights. The group in Hessdalen, Norway, led by Erling Peter Strand, have collected spectra from Earth Lights seen in that location. Dr. Karl Stephan, Professor of Engineering at Texas State University, and I, have experimented with commercial laboratory spectrometers in Mitchell Flat. In addition, I have used various self-designed spectroscopes. By the end of my investigation, I had developed a calibrated spectroscope that was effective and easy to use. Unfortunately, this development could not be fully exploited before the investigation ended.

10. There were several pictures [at your website], taken at night, that had "rainbows" in the pictures. Aren't [creation of] rainbows [only possible] if the light [passes] though something prismatic? Prisms, cut diamonds, raindrops or mist does that. Was it [a] wet night [when] those pictures were taken? I don't understand how those rainbows are made; I thought light had to be white to refract?
A: Early in my investigation, I employed a simple spectroscope technique that consisted of Mylar diffraction material inserted between the lens and the camera. **Figure 32** and **33** (they are #68 and #69 at my www.marfatxlights.com website) referred to in the above question, were made in 2004 using this Mylar technique to parse ML frequencies and display them as part of the image. This simple device was sufficient to distinguish between plasma and non-plasma light sources but was not sophisticated enough to identify chemical elements. Late in the investigation, while employing a more sophisticated glass-diffraction grating spectroscope, I did manage to locate a few line-spectra cases indicative of plasma. However, detailed analysis of these spectra showed them to be plasma headlamps (the age of automobile plasma headlamps is upon us).

The bottom-line: Those rainbow patterns seen in the 2004 pictures (ref. **Figure 32** and **33**) are ML spectra created in my camera lens using Mylar diffraction grating material. I cannot speak for other locations worldwide, but MLs for which I have obtained spectra, have been indicative of chemical fires, not plasma. Reasons for this result are discussed in the chapter, *"What Are Those Lights?"* And finally, spectral analysis is possible with any light source that consists of multiple frequencies.

Marfa Lights History

11. How long have people been seeing these lights?
A: The View Park plaque located in front of the shelter states that long before arrival of European settlers, Native Americans were seeing the lights and believed them to be stars that had fallen to earth. This would be a logical conclusion because they were also seeing meteors entering the atmosphere over what would become known as Mitchell Flat.

Worldwide Locations

12. Where else in the world are similar phenomena seen?
A: Remarkable light phenomena are seen throughout the world. In his paper "*A Scientific Approach to the Investigation of Anomalous Atmospheric Light Phenomena,*" 2010, Dr. Massimo Teodorani listed fourteen locations of similar phenomena worldwide that he had visited in his study of "Earth Lights." See the References list of this book for two of Dr. Teodorani's papers.

Another excellent source of information on worldwide light phenomena are books written and published by William R. Corliss, including the following:
-- *Lightning, Auroras, Nocturnal Lights, and Related Phenomena.* Glen Arm, MD: The Sourcebook Project, 1982.
-- *Remarkable Luminous Phenomena In Nature: A Catalog of Geophysical Anomalies.* Glen Arm, MD: The Sourcebook Project, 2001.

Camping Requests

13. Can I camp overnight at the View Park?
A: The Marfa Lights View Park is a roadside rest area and is not intended for overnight camping. I have noticed that people with recreational vehicles, campers, and large trucks do sometimes stay very late, perhaps overnight, but they must be fully self-supporting because there are no hookups or provisions for extended stay. Before considering any kind of overnight stay, please contact the Texas Department of Transportation in Alpine at (915) 837-3391.

An excellent place that does support camping is the Texas State Park in Fort Davis (915) 426-3254. The park also includes Indian Lodge, a small hotel with beautiful rooms, vistas, and great American and Texas style food. The dining room is available to campers as well. There are also RV camps in both Marfa and Alpine.

Emergencies

14. What should I do if I see people damaging the facility, applying graffiti, or committing other illegal acts?
A: The View Park is located in Presidio County. To contact the County Sheriff's office, call (432) 229-3204.

15. Who do I call in the event of a medical emergency?
A: Emergency Medical Services in Marfa are at 113 Highland Avenue, (432) 729-3151. In Alpine, call Big Bend Regional Medical Center, (432) 837-3447, 2600 N. Highway 118.

General Questions

**16. There is a small building with an odd white cone-shaped roof a couple of miles west of Marfa Lights Park. Is this some kind of instrumentation connected to the Marfa Lights?

A: No. The building is an FAA VORTAC station used as a navigation aid for aircraft.

17. What is the small white building just south of the Marfa Lights View Park?

A: It appears to be an enclosure for a well pump. Because this house is painted white, it reflects passing car lights. On a dark night, people who have not seen the pump house and are unaware of its presence sometimes mistake these reflections as mystery lights.

18. I noticed an object hanging in the sky in the direction of Marfa. After dark it had a strobe light. Is this some sort of advertising blimp?

A: The object is a blimp flown by the United States Air Force. It carries radar used to search for aircraft crossing our southern border (the Rio Grande River). The blimp is attached to the ground but can be flown as high as 10,000 feet.

19. The odd lights I saw were vertical columns of light. They looked like search lights, but were vertical, maybe 30 feet high, and they would fade from view in a fairly short time. Were these Marfa Lights?

A: What you were seeing may well have been latent images -- a sensory aftereffect -- of telephone poles or roof support poles. Staring intently into the night when searching for MLs can cause images to "stick" in your visual system. Move your head left or right and the stuck (latent) image appears in your field of view. This phenomena is more likely to happen during twilight before the evening darkness makes telephone poles less obvious. If you have this experience, try staring intently at something else, and then move your head to look for the latent image. The effect (latent image), if it is one, will be gone.

20. Where in Mitchell Flat were your automated night cameras located?

A: My decision has been to not provide specific locations for those investigation assets in order to protect ranch owners from the many inquiries that would be certain to follow. Here are the reasons:

(1) I owe much to ranch owners who, in return for no tangible benefit, not only accommodated my personal and equipment intrusions, but helped me in every way possible. Their trust in me and their generosity were, and are, greatly appreciated. Those night camera stations were absolutely essential. Without them, my investigation would have been forced to end very early with limited results. It is important to understand that these wonderful people are ranchers, period. They were not involved directly in the investigation.

(2) All cameras have been removed; there is nothing left to see.

(3) Filling this book with thousands of position uncertainty calculations, and low resolution black and white photographs would make for a dull, uninteresting book. Instead, I have elected to provide direction and distance vectors from the View Park because data in that form is simple and more useful to those who have an interest in knowing where these lights were located.

21. Where are the fault lines in Mitchell Flat?

A: Thanks to Harvey Howell and Sunup Oil, I am able to share that information in **Map 3,** Chapter 2.

Chapter 6

Best Evidence for Mystery Lights

Figure 18. Field telescopes and spectrometer waiting for darkness in Mitchell Flat

Fascinating as the accounts in Chapter 1 may be, skeptics treat all stories in a dismissive way, asserting that nothing is more suspect than eyewitness testimony offered to a gullible public without a shred of evidence. Sworn eyewitness accounts are accepted by our legal system, but it is true that eyewitness accounts, in general, are often conflicting and unreliable. So it is fair to ask, "What evidence does Bunnell have that Marfa Lights are anything more than misidentification of car lights and/or other explainable light sources?" In this chapter, I present my best evidence in the form of high resolution color photographs along with location and time information derived from automated night cameras, plus observation details recorded on site after each event. This chapter includes previously unpublished photographs and details from seven selected ML nights, including, to the extent they are known, times, locations, and directions of travel. These seven nights are selective samples from a larger collection of data.

For the convenience of those planning trips to Marfa, start and end locations of these detected MLs are provided, when possible, as magnetic vectors from the View Park. Appendix provides details regarding computed location uncertainties.

Evolution of Data Collection Methods

Being someone who grew up in Presidio County and graduated from Marfa High School, I was well aware of mysterious Marfa Lights, and had tried looking for them a few times. But it was the two nights in November, 2000, as related in Chapter 1 (HML account #10), that woke me up to the fact that these phenomena were not only very real, but worthy of serious investigation. Unable to find any satisfactory explanations in local libraries or at nearby Sul Ross University, I decided to do my own investigation. I anticipated spending a month or two at most of my newly begun retirement. Had I known what lay ahead of me, I would not have started this endeavor, but now that it is history, I am very glad to have done it. The purpose of this book is to share what I learned about this intriguing phenomena.

The biggest obstacle to learning anything about these mysterious lights is the scarcity of their appearances (at least during the time of my investigation). It is certainly understandable that many smart people have visited Marfa hoping to see them, but came away concluding, incorrectly, that mysterious lights do not exist. They have seen nothing more than excited people watching distant car lights. I started my investigation with the considerable benefit of having experienced an unmistakable ML show and I was, therefore, armed with necessary tolerance to wait for their next appearance.

The problem was that I live hundreds of miles from Marfa and my initial "hit-or-miss" approach quickly proved impractical. What was needed was a way to predict when they would next appear. Seeking some pattern of appearances, I installed an automated video camera system (Roofus) on the ranch of a friend. Roofus was designed to run nightly and save recorded video to a removable hard drive. I would take a reformatted hard drive with me on each Marfa visit and swap out the loaded hard drive, returning home with data that I would review when I had time, prior to scheduling the next trip.

Unfortunately, trip after trip, no pattern of appearances emerged. But Roofus proved useful in another way. Whenever I was fortunate enough to see an ML from the View Park, I would check to see if Roofus had also photographed it. I could then use triangulation to calculate the ML's location. Since this only worked for periods of time when I was observing from the View Park, I added another recording station, Snoopy, opening the door to ML triangulations anytime both automated monitoring stations acquired the same target, even if I was many miles away.

The problem with this arrangement was that Mitchell Flat is a large region. Overlapping Roofus and Snoopy fields of view accounted for only a small percentage of Mitchell Flat. I badly needed more night cameras, especially in the Southeast quadrant where MLs seemed more likely to appear. In 2006, thanks to the interest, trust, and graciousness of two ranch owners, it became possible to add two more monitoring stations, Owlbert A and B. By the end of that year, I was routinely using nine to ten fully automated monitoring stations yielding much more information than would ever have been possible without these added camera stations. The downside was that reviewing collected video became a huge burden soaking up all of my time. The upside was that reviewing all those videos provided a lot of insight into light sources, ranch vehicle patterns, ML behaviors, and ML locations.

Each Marfa trip to collect monitoring station data provided an opportunity to spend 3 or 4 nights observing in person with an ability to take high resolution color photography of any MLs that made an appearance. Returning home, I would then use the hard drives I had retrieved to help analyze and better understand any ML activity I had been able to photograph during my Marfa visit. In this chapter I present detailed photographs collected by me (hands on) during seven nights between 2003 and 2007. Time, direction, and distance data are included to the extent possible drawing on video data from my monitoring stations. In my best judgement, these lights were neither man-made nor mirages. They were genuinely mysterious lights in Mitchell Flat.

February 19, 2003: First Capture of ML Details

On this cold, windy night I was fortunate enough to capture three clear ML photographs. This may have been the closest I have been to an ML. I was close enough for a zoom lens to reveal exactly what the ML was doing in exquisite detail (**Figures 19, 20, and 21**). **Figure 19** graces the cover of this book and captures On/Off states of illumination as well as ongoing combustive processes. **Figures 20** and **21** show clear evidence of energy decay as the ML continued westward and went out. These remarkable photographs reveal much about the true nature of MLs, a subject that will be discussed in the next chapter.

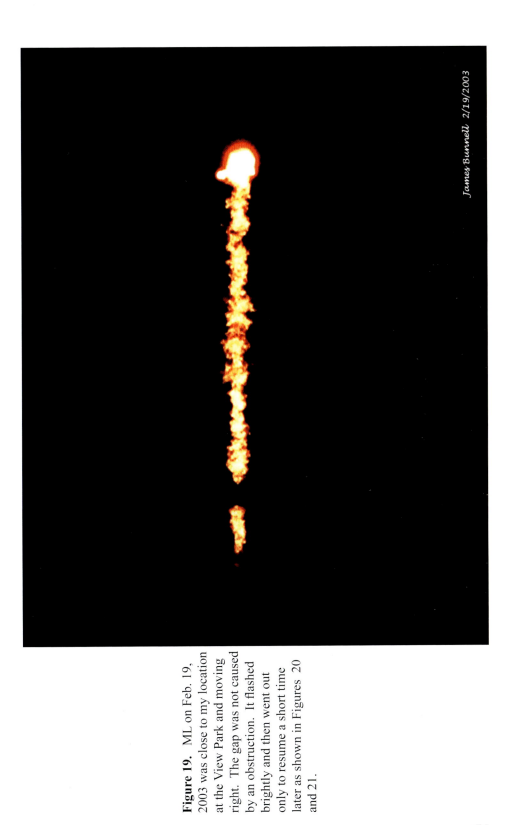

James Bunnell 2/19/2003

Figure 19. ML on Feb. 19, 2003 was close to my location at the View Park and moving right. The gap was not caused by an obstruction. It flashed brightly and then went out only to resume a short time later as shown in Figures 20 and 21.

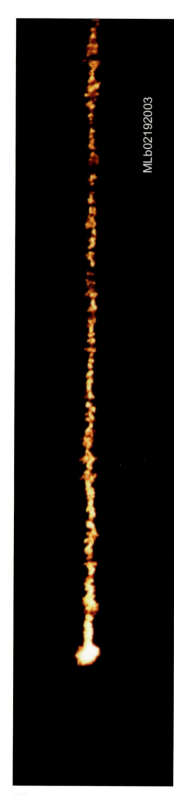

Figure 20. ML on Feb. 19, 2003 came back on with a flash and continued its journey to the right.

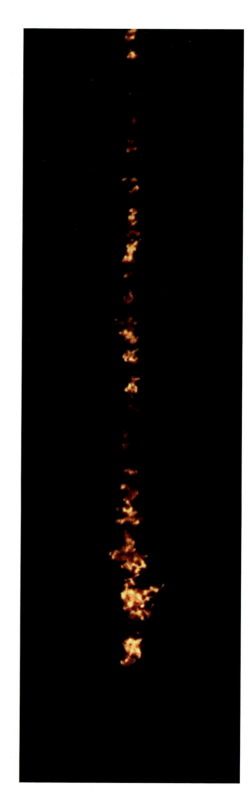

Figure 21. Zoomed image on Feb. 19, 2003 shows how ML becomes more elongated, fainter, and then goes out.

To my naked eyes, this ML appeared as a ball of yellow/orange light that turned On/Off and flashed brightly twice as it flew westward. The zoom lens used on that occasion penetrated the ball of light to reveal a complex energy event. I was amazed and pleased to discover that there was so much more to these incredibly mysterious lights than I had previously realized.

02/19/2003 Details

Sunset (PM CST):	6:46
Moon:	Not up
Start (PM CST):	**8:20**
ML duration:	**Estimated ~ 10 minutes.**
Direction at start:	174 deg. magnetic
Direction at end:	186 deg. magnetic
Distance from VP:	Unknown
Travel Distance:	Unknown
Travel speed:	Unknown
Camera Location:	N30 deg. 16.499 min. W103 deg. 53.067 min.
Camera Type:	Pentax ZX-30 (35 mm color film) SLR
Camera Lens:	Tamron AF70-300 mm F/4-5.6
Camera Mount:	Tripod, remote shutter release (always)
Auto night camera:	ML was too far north to be seen by Roofus
Temperature:	48.2 deg. F.
Humidity:	48%
Precipitation:	None
Wind Direction:	NE
Wind Speed:	14 mph
Visibility:	9 miles

All three of these images, and others published in this book, are actually "light tracks" created by ML movement during the time that the camera shutter was open (camera selected exposure times were not available for these film cameras, but they were all long exposures).

Figure 19 reveals three important details:

1) There is evidence of two distinct gaps created by the light being in an Off state during the exposure. The left gap was already started when the camera shutter opened. A second shorter gap is obvious near the left end of the light track.

2) The light track reveals "explosive like" behavior suggesting some kind of combustive process is occurring.

3) The first frame ends with the bright flash that I had observed followed by the light going out. This sudden burst of energy produced a step-change in brightness that was momentary as the light then went out (or was blown out). It is tempting to surmise that the bright flash may have been a more "fuel-rich" condition, given the small ejected portion visible near the top of the flash (**Figure 19**).

After repositioning my camera and starting a second exposure, the ML reappeared (**Figure 20**) in perfect alignment with its prior trajectory and continued moving westward. A careful examination of the image reveals evidence of energy decay, with the process becoming a little less bright and slightly more elongated near the right end of the exposure. This process of decay becomes more obvious in the third photograph. The third photograph (**Figure 21**) has been digitally zoomed to show greater detail and there is clear evidence that the light track is becoming less energetic, less bright, more elongated, and then the ML exhausts before I can collect a fourth image.

Comment:

These pictures provide useful insight into the nature of MLs:

1) MLs probably start with a given amount of energy and experience energy decay as they move and generate visible displays.

2) Generated displays look like combustion processes, possibly

oxidation as they interact with the atmosphere. This is consistent with later collected continuous spectral profiles.

3) These combustion-like processes should be generating sound waves, but there are no reports of MLs generating sound within the range of human hearing. I heard no sound on this occasion (nor have I with any ML event). Given the level of camera recorded detail, I suspect this was probably the closest that I have been to an ML.

How do I know these were not vehicle headlights or a mirage?

These photographs provide sufficient detail to exclude either type of light source. Ongoing combustive processes and the two bright flashes are uncharacteristic of automotive headlamps. Has anyone ever seen a headlight video that displays similar combustive patterns? **Figures 20** and **21** show clear evidence of energy decay by exhibiting less intensity and more elongation as a function of time and distance until the light source finally goes out. This observed decay is inconsistent with car lights or mirages. Without question, there are night mirages in Mitchell Flat (they are discussed in Chapter 8) but these dynamic displays with evidence of energy decay as the ML moves right do not lend themselves to a mirage explanation.

Where was the event?

I have directions and approximate event times but do not know how far from the View Park this ML might have been. Given the unusual clarity of the three images, it had to be close to my location. Based on stories related in the previous chapter, other observers have experienced closer encounters (e.g., Charlotte Allen, Strange Lights stories 2 &3).

May 7, 2003: Flight of Two Complex MLs

Approximately half an hour after sunset an ML flared to brightness southeast of my location at the View Park. It was brighter than mercury vapor ranch lights and brighter than all other visible light sources. Before I could locate it in the view finder of one of my tripod mounted cameras, it dimmed and went out. Fifty minutes later at 9:55:34 PM CDT the light reappeared, or else it was a new ML in a different location. It was being photographed from miles away by my automated nighttime monitoring station Roofus (**Figure 22**).

I also photographed it from the View Park (**Figure 23**). This second appearance lasted about two minutes with the ML performing some kind of motion while the camera shutter was open. There would be two separate MLs on this night so I will refer to this first photograph as ML1

Figure 22. In 2003, the View looking over the top of Roofus' camera housing toward Goat Mountain. Cathedral mountain is on the left. Tree was later trimmed to provide better views to the SE.

Figure 23. ML1a on May 7, 2003 lasted a couple of minutes and then went out. It was moving back and forth and was too bright to miss.

and give it a sub-designation of "a" to represent the first recorded appearance of ML1. Knowing the vector direction from automated video station Roofus, plus the direction from my location at the view park, it is possible to know where ML1a was located (15 miles from my location) and, thanks to US topography data, it is possible to also know the elevation of terrain below ML1a was 5017 feet. After the photograph in **Figure 23** was taken, the light went out and returned at 9:58:50 PM CDT in a new location (ML1b) to create an interesting display with both left and right directions of travel (**Figure 24**). Vertical variation in the light track suggests that the ML might have been trying to spiral. Similar light-track patterns were recorded multiple times as ML1 continued traveling to the northwest.

The next photograph I took that evening would be of a second ML. ML2 started with an interesting flat pattern of movement that looked like a collection of smaller MLs orbiting a parent ML (**Figure 25**). It could not be determined for certain if that was the case, or if this was a single ML shuttling left and right. Two traces of light can be seen in **Figure 25**

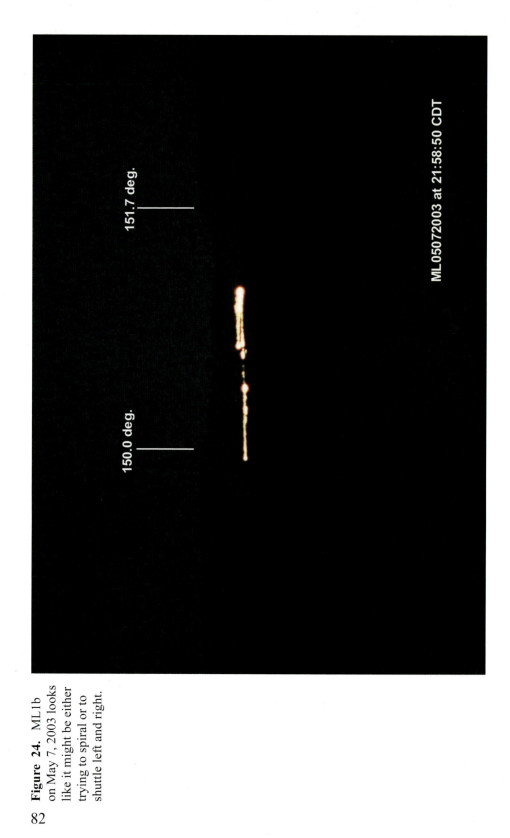

Figure 24. ML1b on May 7, 2003 looks like it might be either trying to spiral or to shuttle left and right.

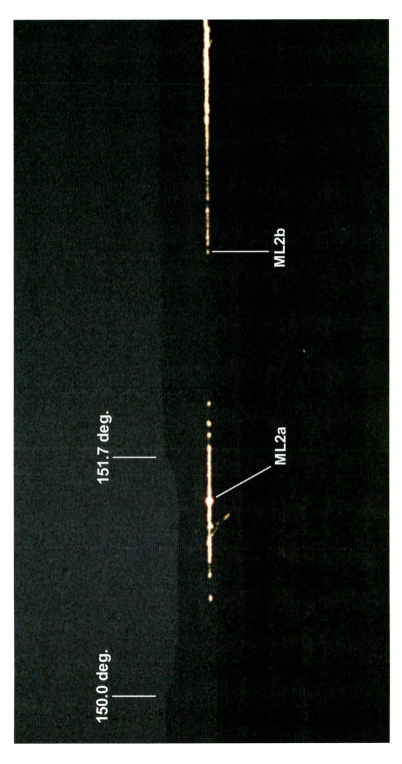

Figure 25. ML2a on May 7, 2003 is either orbiting offspring or else they are shuttling left and right. Light tracks of two ejected particles provide clues to the ML's altitude above terrain. ML2b continued on for many miles.

extending downward from this light track pattern. When discussing this figure in ***Hunting Marfa Lights,*** I assumed that these were small orbiting ML offspring that lost energy and were photographed as they fell toward the ground. Today, for reasons explained in the next chapter, I would say these excursions were more likely to have been ejected burning material. Instead of falling toward the ground, they are more likely to have been expelled in unknown directions.

A long shutter exposure recorded light tracks made by both MLs as they flew past the central mercury vapor (CMV) ranch light (**Figure 26**). That CMV was mounted on a 28-foot pole (both of the mercury vapor lamps shown in **Figure 26** have since stopped illuminating) and as the MLs passed near that location they appeared to be slightly lower than the CMV. While ML altitudes cannot be precisely determined, I estimate they were approximately 20 feet above local terrain.

The image shown in **Figure 27** enabled calculation of how far west these MLs traveled before they slowed and then went out. ML1b traveled a minimum straight line distance of 9.78 miles in 8 minutes 33 seconds for an average speed of 69 mph. Actual speed was greater because, based on Roofus direction and time data, ML1b did not travel in a straight line; it followed a curving route to the north as illustrated in **Map 6**. Based on a straight line distance, ML2 traveled a minimum of 8.92 miles in 7 minutes 57 seconds for an average speed of 67 mph, but ML2's actual speed was greater because it also followed a non-straight path (**Map 6**).

Assuming that ML paths plotted in **Map 6** are valid approximations, what forces would account for directional changes in their routes? Given that these MLs were flying above the ground, wind forces would normally be the explanation. Wind was blowing from the southeast at about 4.6 mph, as measured at the airport, and both MLs traveled northwest, a direction consistent with prevailing wind. However, the two path trajectories are much different even though they were both in flight at about the same time. How could the wind have caused one path to curve to the north while the other ML followed a weaving-wandering course to

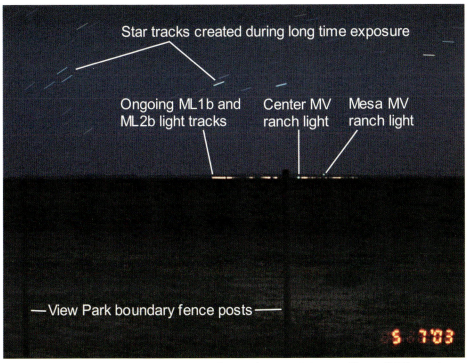

Figure 26. ML1 and 2 light tracks passing near Mercury Vapor (MV) ranch lights May 7, 2003.

Figure 27. Image shows how far MLs 1 and 2 traveled before going out.

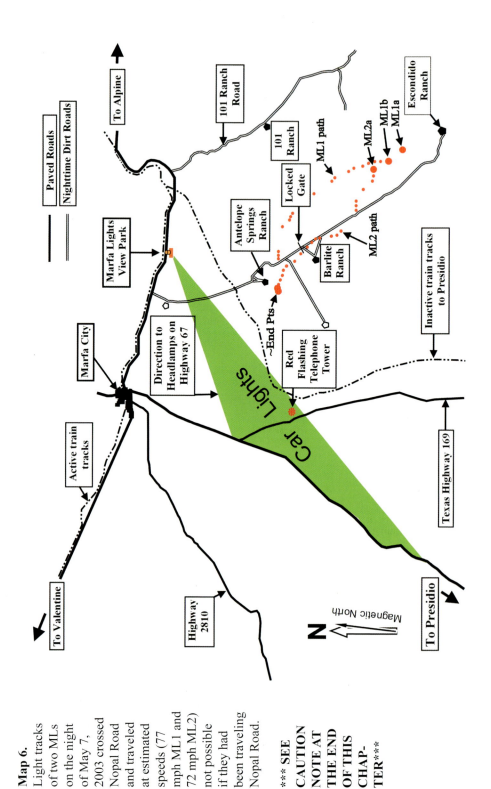

Map 6. Light tracks of two MLs on the night of May 7, 2003 crossed Nopal Road and traveled at estimated speeds (77 mph ML1 and 72 mph ML2) not possible if they had been traveling Nopal Road.

*** SEE CAUTION NOTE AT THE END OF THIS CHAPTER***

the same general destination as shown in **Map 6**? It should also be noted that stationary MLs observed previously on very windy nights exhibited absolutely no wind response whatsoever (See Chapter 1 ML stories, SL#1, HML #10, and HML #13). It seems more likely that recorded route variations are caused by some other force or combination of forces.

Altitude Calculations

Based on the triangulated location (Roofus and bearing from my position at the View Park), it was possible to use US topography data to determine terrain elevation under ML2a (~4861 feet) [note: the ~ symbol as used in this book means approximately] and elevation of the background horizon along my line of sight from the View Park (~5310 feet). The difficulty with finding picture-specific altitudes has to do with locating that 4861-foot ground spot beneath the ML in **Figure 25**. Ordinarily this task would be difficult because the terrain is covered with brush as it slopes upward toward the background mesa, providing no good visual clues regarding terrain height in the photograph. Fortunately this particular section of ML2's light track provides unique information in the form of downward trajectories created by two expelled particles (**Figure 25**) that were evidently ejected as the ML was traveling to the northwest. If these trajectory excursions were created by ejected material, then their true direction and extent is unknown, but their vertical component (~168 feet) can be measured from the photograph and used to establish minimum altitude of the ML source. This is a minimum altitude above terrain because the ejected particles may have extinguished before reaching the ground.

I know from **Figure 26** that ML altitudes were on the order of 20 feet above terrain when they flew past the CMV light. What accounts for this loss of ~ 148 feet in altitude as these MLs traveled approximately 6.1 miles to the Northwest? Could it be that ML altitudes are tied to the strength of inherent magnetic fields (potential for magnetic fields is discussed in Chapter 7) and that those magnetic fields reduce in strength over time because energy is being consumed generating ML displays?

But if ML2 lost 148 feet (more or less) traveling 6.1 statute miles from its initial position to where it passed near the center mercury vapor light, then there should be evidence of a downward sloping trajectory. There is evidence of this, but the downward slope is only 0.26 of a degree, a slope difficult to discern in **Figures 25** and **26**.

05/07/2003 Details		ML1	ML2
Sunset (PM CDT):	8:36		
Moon:	was up		
Start (PM CDT):		9:55:34	10:02:30
ML duration (total):	00:15:49		
05/07/2003 Details		**ML1**	**ML2**
Direction to MLs at start:		150 deg. mag.	151.5 deg. mag.
Distance from VP at start:		15 miles	13 miles
Travel times (MLb segments):		00:08:33	00:07:57
Straight line distances		9.78 miles	8.92 miles
Speeds if straight line		69 mph	67 mph
Estimated line distances		10.92 miles	9.57 miles
Speeds based on est. distances		77 mph	72 mph

Camera locations:	N30 deg. 16.499 min, W103 deg. 53.067 min.
Cameras:	Pentax ZX-30 (2)
Camera lenses:	Tamron AF70-300 mm and Pentax 35-80 mm
Camera mounts:	Tripods & remote shutter release on both
Auto night camera:	Roofus used for triangulation and event times

Temp. at start:	71.6 deg. F.
Humidity:	11%
Precipitation:	None
Wind direction:	SE
Wind speed:	4.6 mph
Visibility:	10 miles

How do I know these were not vehicle headlights or a mirage?

It is not possible that these light patterns were made by vehicles traveling on Nopal Road (the only dirt road anywhere near the right location) because calculated straight line speeds are too great for prevailing road conditions (and they did not travel in straight lines) plus the fact that any such trip would have required two stops at the locked gate on Nopal Road. Today the locked gate on Nopal can be opened remotely (like a garage door), but in 2003 it was strictly a manual gate secured with padlocks. Passage through the gate required exiting one's vehicle to open and remove the padlock. Then the gate had to be manually opened. More time would be required to get back into the vehicle and drive through the open gate. Then it would be necessary to exit the vehicle again in order to close the gate and re-lock it. This was, altogether, a time consuming process totally inconsistent with recorded ML transit times. But even if the gate had been standing wide open, using Nopal road to make such a nighttime trip would have required excessive speeds not possible on a pothole filled dirt ranch road. Computed ML positions do not correspond to Nopal Road and there are no other roads that could have been used by vehicles to make such a trip. Moreover **Figures 24** and **25**, taken by me from the View Park, include altitudes (at least 168 feet above local terrain in one case), computed locations, and trajectories of expelled elements (**Figure 25**) that are inconsistent with vehicle lights.

Particle ejections and long curving complex display patterns, recorded from widely separated locations (View Park and Roofus), are inconsistent with a mirage explanation.

May 8, 2003: ML Explodes

Two more traveling MLs appeared the next night in May, 2003. The light track of the first ML (the numbering convention I am using is per night, so the first ML on any night is ML1 and the second ML is ML2) included a significant display gap while flying well above local terrain as evidenced by falling material, and the ML's height relative to background mesas that are approximately 500 feet above Mitchell Flat. After the gap, it resumed visual display with time, speed, and direction unaltered by its off-state, suggesting that something unseen must have continued through the gap. This was perhaps the most "explosive" ML event ever recorded by my cameras. Burning material from the explosion can be seen descending toward the ground on a slanted trajectory indicating that the particles have mass and momentum (**Figure 28** and **29**). **This explosive event eliminates both cars lights and mirage conditions as valid explanations.**

From my southwest plaque observation point at the View Park, it seemed as if ML1 returned a short time later and continued its travel to the northwest, but what continued was actually a second ML with a starting point located east of where ML1 extinguished (**Figure 30**). ML2 continued across Nopal Road and traveled ~12 miles before going out near the inactive Presidio railroad tracks (**Map 7**). Average speed, if ML2 had been traveling in a straight line, would have been 52 mph, however, Roofus time and direction data (**Map 7**), shows ML2 followed a wandering path similar to ML2 from the prior night and was therefore traveling faster than 52 mph. If this May 8th ML2 had been someone driving northwest on Nopal Road, significant time would have been required to pass through the locked gate on Nopal Road and that would have required excessive speeds not feasible at night on a dirt ranch road.

05/08/2003 Details		ML1	ML2
Sunset (PM CDT):	8:37		
Moon:	Not up		
Start (PM CDT):		10:15:55	10:19:38
Direction to MLs at start:		149.2 deg. m.	150.2 deg. m.
Distance from VP at start:		15 miles	13 miles

Figure 28. ML1 on May 8, 2003 followed an ascending trajectory with a prominent gap. There are no possible obstructions to explain this gap made while the ML was high above terrain as evidenced by falling material at the explosive end.

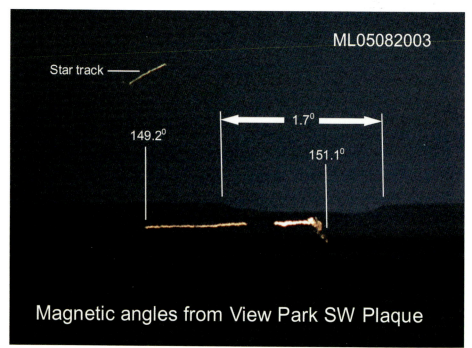

Figure 29. ML1 background mesas were used to determine vectors from my camera location at the View Park southwest plaque. Camera lens was 300 mm; time exposure was 42 seconds.

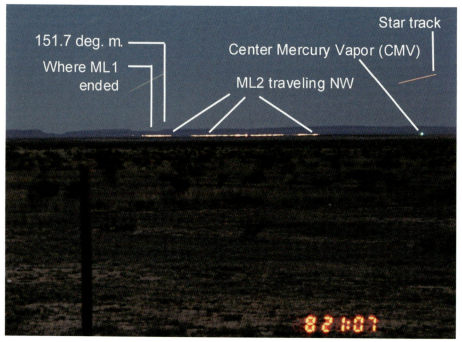

Figure 30. Pentax camera with 80 mm lens captures start of ML2 east of where ML1 ended. Lens was 80 mm; exposure time was 7' 6" resulting in much brighter picture.

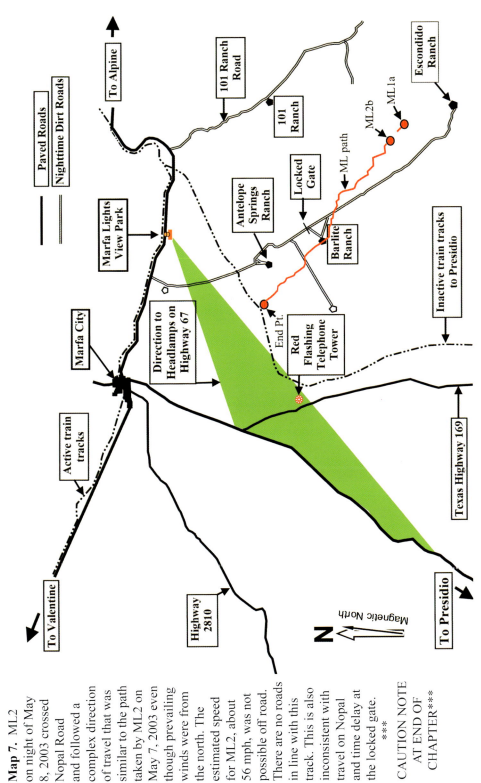

Map 7. ML2 on night of May 8, 2003 crossed Nopal Road and followed a complex direction of travel that was similar to the path taken by ML2 on May 7, 2003 even though prevailing winds were from the north. The estimated speed for ML2, about 56 mph, was not possible off road. There are no roads in line with this track. This is also inconsistent with travel on Nopal and time delay at the locked gate.

***

CAUTION NOTE AT END OF CHAPTER***

Travel times:	00:02:20	00:13:57
Straight line travel:		12 miles
Speed if straight line:		~ 52 mph
Estimated speed if not straight line:		~ 56 mph

Camera location:	N30 deg. 16.499 min, W103 deg. 53.067 min.
Cameras:	Pentax ZX-30 (2)
Camera lenses:	Tamron AF70-300 mm and Pentax 35-80 mm
Auto night camera:	Roofus used for triangulation and event times

Temp. at start:	62.6 deg. F.
Humidity:	11%
Precipitation:	None
Wind direction:	N
Wind speed:	10.4 mph
Visibility:	10 miles

Comment

General direction of travel was to the northwest (**Map 7**). Wind direction on this night was from the north at 10.4 mph. If this ML was wind driven, it should have been moving south instead of northwest.

May 8, 2004: Multiple MLs

A year later, also on May 8th (by coincidence), multiple MLs would once again entertain with stunning displays. The first May 8th ML appeared soon after dark with me looking in the opposite direction while giving an impromptu talk to a group of college students who had arrived by bus. When one of the students called this first ML to my attention, I was skeptical. But my initial skepticism quickly vanished as I watched a pulsing, intensely bright light skipping along just above the desert creosote

Figure 31. 2nd ML on May 8, 2004 was located close to the View Park

brush.

    I had begun talking to these enjoyable college students without taking time to unload and set up camera equipment. Rushing back to my truck, I extracted a telescope, camera and tripod. By the time I could get everything set up, the no-notice ML had gone out, but there was already another in sight and closer. It lasted long enough for me to take a time exposure (**Figure 31**). The wind was blowing with such force that I feared even my heavy equipment would be blown down, possibly breaking the camera and/or telescope. Even though I had started a second exposure, I grabbed my entire setup and carried everything into the View Park Pavilion where they were protected from wind by a wall, thereby spoiling the second exposure. The second ML disappeared soon after. Almost immediately a third ML appeared to the southeast. This third ML was further away (14 miles), but it was bright and pulsing On/Off in typical ML fashion. This third event lasted three minutes and fifty-four seconds, long enough for me to obtain three time exposures. The best two are presented in **Figures 32** and **33**. **Figure 34** is a composite of all three photographs with directional information included. The composite photograph shows this last ML moving left and down as seen from the View Park but, thanks to monitoring station Roofus, I know that the ML actually traveled mostly NNW as shown in **Map 8**. Actual path between the start and end points is not known.

    The camera used to take all of these photographs was equipped to obtain ML spectra using a Mylar diffraction grating insert between the telescopic lens and the camera. For some unknown reason, the camera did not capture any spectra for the first photograph (**Figure 31**). The remaining figures do include spectra that shows as multi-colored (rainbow-like) patterns. These early spectra were uncalibrated, but nevertheless reveal continuous spectra indicative of chemical combustion process rather than plasma (see Chapter 7 for a discussion of possible ML construction and origins).

    Roofus did not capture either of the first two MLs, confirming that

Figure 32. ML3b on May 8, 2004. The rainbow patterns are the ML's spectra. This was captured in my camera by using a Mylar diffraction grating insert.

Figure 33. ML3c on May 8, 2004. These rainbow spectra are continuous, indicating chemical combustion rather than plasma.

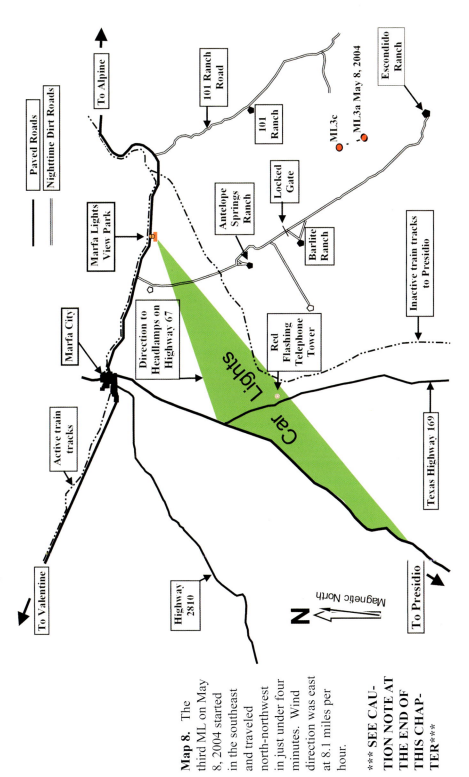

Map 8. The third ML on May 8, 2004 started in the southeast and traveled north-northwest in just under four minutes. Wind direction was east at 8.1 miles per hour.

*** SEE CAUTION NOTE AT THE END OF THIS CHAPTER ***

they were located north of Roofus' field of view and therefore closer to the View Park. That the first photograph was fairly close to the View Park seems apparent in **Figure 31**. ML2 is flying west higher than and near a post in the View Park boundary fence.

5/8/2004 Details		ML2	ML3
Sunset (PM CDT):	8:38		
Moon:	Not up		
Start (PM CDT):	9:04:31		
ML duration:			ML3 3' 54"
Directions to MLs at start:		South of VP	ML3 148.8 deg. mag.
Distance from View Park(miles):			ML3 = ~ 14 miles

Camera location:	N30 deg. 16.468 min, W103 deg. 51.939 min.
Cameras:	Pentax ZX-30
Camera lenses:	Celestron C5 Schmidt-Cassegrain, 127 mm
Camera mounts:	Remote shutter release
Auto night camera:	Roofus; triangulation and event times
Temp. at start:	68.9 deg. F.

Figure 34. A composite image showing ML3 positions from three photographs on May 8, 2004. With respect to the background mesas, ML3 moved to a lower altitude, first left and then right, then left again as seen from the View Park.

Humidity:	37%
Precipitation:	None
Wind direction:	E
Wind speed:	8.1 mph
Visibility:	10 miles

How do I know these were not headlights of a vehicle on the Mesa?

Based on Roofus data and direction from the View Park, the third ML was located far short of background mesas (**Map 8**) and clearly flying well above local terrain eliminating any possibility that these light tracks were being generated by vehicle headlights.

That ML spectra indicated chemical combustion processes was surprising because observed ML behaviors are extremely diverse (each ML event is unique). Many exhibit long lifetimes, especially considering the energy of their displays. In addition, they seem unaffected by wind, appear to be silent, and are able to travel close to the ground. All of these rather exotic characteristics should be indicators of plasma, and yet these spectra seemed to indicate otherwise. I will offer a possible explanation for this odd dichotomy in Chapter 7.

August 11, 2006: Shooting Over the Gate

On this August night I elected to end watching for MLs close to midnight and was driving north on a private ranch road to reach the main ranch road, Nopal, when I noticed an unexpected orange light off to my right. It was at higher elevation than my location, but I assumed it was a ranch house on a hill side and made a mental note to take a location bearing after reaching the locked gate on Nopal Road. As I stopped at the gate, I retrieved my compass-equipped binoculars, but the light had gone out. I put the binoculars back into my truck, proceeded to unlock the gate, open it, and drive through. After securing the lock on the gate, I looked south and saw the light was on again. It then turned off and back on. Oh my gosh! This was no ranch house; it was an ML and there I stood on the wrong side of a locked gate, with all of my equipment stored in the truck!

As fast as possible, I extracted a Canon Digital SLR camera, a telescope and tripod. I began taking pictures sixteen minutes after midnight, shooting over the locked gate. I managed to take about a dozen pictures before the ML went out. The best images are shown in two composites, **Figures 35** and **36**.

After the ML went out without coming back on, I tried to find it using a night vision device, but had no success. Direction to the ML was 145 degrees magnetic from where my camera was located at the locked gate. Not convinced that the ML was out for good, I unlocked the gate, drove through, and re-locked the gate. The ML had appeared to be somewhere close to background mesas, so I drove south on Nopal Road attempting to get as close as possible to its location; I was hoping it might reappear. About five miles from those background mesas, Nopal Road takes a small jog east and enters Escondido Ranch. Because I had not asked permission to be on that ranch, it was necessary to stop my southbound journey at that point. Unable to proceed, I pulled out a hand meter and was amazed to see a magnetic flux density disturbance of 49.1 milligauss. A residual field disturbance this elevated was unusual. Previous measurements of the magnetic field along Nopal Road had shown an average variation of 1.7 milligauss. Might this magnetic disturbance have resulted from or be related to that night's ML? I suspect it was, but my investigation of MLs has been limited to visual and infrared frequencies. Exploration of other frequencies is needed.

At a much later date, I had time to analyze video collected by my automated night camera, Owlbert A (**Figure 37**), and calculate the intersection of my directional vector from the locked gate and another vector from Owlbert A. The calculation revealed that the ML on August 11, 2006 went out at a location about 2300 feet west of where I had stopped and used my field meter (N30 deg., 5.382 min., W103 deg., 49.830 min.). Had

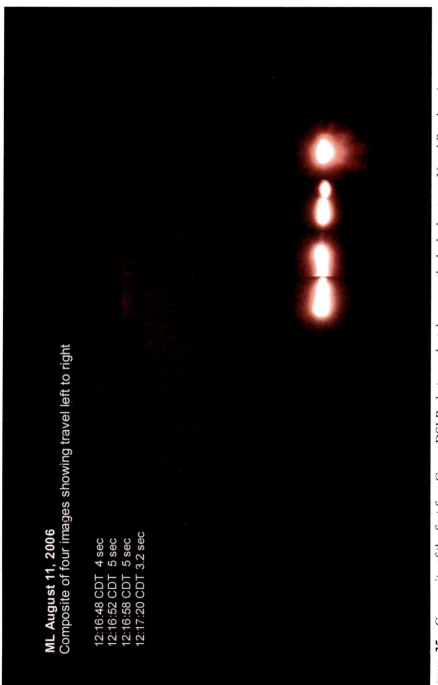

Figure 35. Composite of the first four Canon DSLR photographs taken over the locked gate on Nopal Road on August 11, 2006. The ML was moving left to right with variable display intensity.

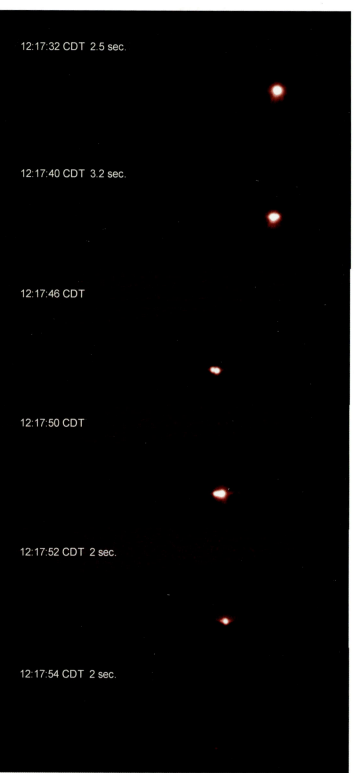

Figure 36. The ML on August 11, 2006, changed directions a couple of times while becoming less intense and then faded out completely.

I known that at the time, I could have turned right and driven even closer to the end spot with ease. It would have been interesting to obtain another meter reading where the ML went out.

Owlbert's video data showed that the ML had a lifetime of four minutes and fifty-eight seconds. Photographs (**Figure 35** and **36**) were taken during the last minute. The residual magnetic disturbance, measured about an hour after the ML went out, lends credibility to the notion that **MLs are fundamentally plasma in origin and that they do create significant magnetic fields that remain in evidence even after chemical surface fires go out.**

Figure 37. Automated Night Camera Owlbert A. The left-front camera, A2, was used to detect an ML on 8/11/2006.

8/11/2006 Details

Sunset (PM CDT):	8:42
Moon:	Was up
Start (AM CDT):	00:02:36

ML duration:	00:04:58
Directions from View Park:	160.3 deg. magnetic
Distance from View Park:	~ 13 miles

Camera location:	N30 deg. 9.46 min, W103 deg. 52.731 min.
Direction from camera:	145 deg. magnetic (from the locked gate)
Distance form camera:	5.34 miles (from the locked gate)
Camera:	Canon DSLR (model 300D with IR filter removed)
Camera lens:	Celestron C5 Schmidt-Cassegrain
Automated camera:	Owlbert A; triangulation and event times

Temp. at start:	66.2 deg. F.
Humidity:	78%
Precipitation:	None
Wind direction:	SSE
Wind speed:	12.7 mph
Visibility:	10 miles

How can I be sure this ML was not vehicle headlights on Nopal Road?
1) Intersection of Owlbert A directional vectors with the 145 degree compass reading taken from the locked gate on Nopal show that the ML, during the time I was photographing it, was located west of Nopal Road, about five miles short of background mesas, and was flying well above the terrain in that location.
2) Vehicle traffic, if any existed, would not account for the measured residual magnetic disturbance, but this disturbance may have been related to the ML.
3) The light is clearly shown to be getting smaller and less bright during the final seconds (**Figure 36**). This slow decay to off is not characteristic of vehicle headlights.
4) Any vehicle driving north on Nopal Road would have been approaching my location and headlights would not have gone out unless the vehicle

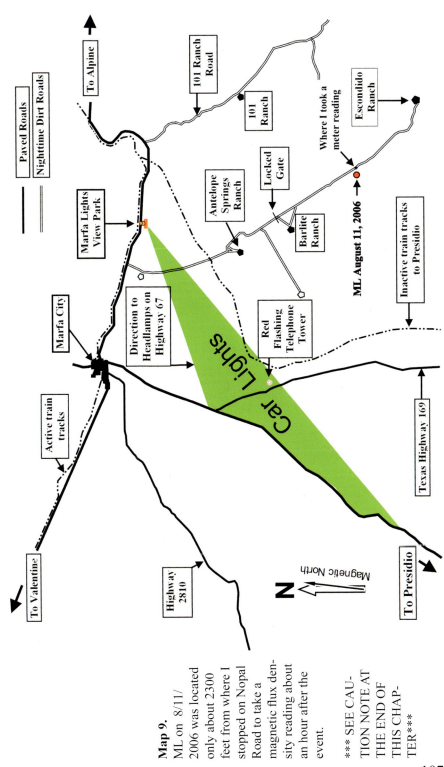

Map 9.
ML on 8/11/2006 was located only about 2300 feet from where I stopped on Nopal Road to take a magnetic flux density reading about an hour after the event.

*** SEE CAUTION NOTE AT THE END OF THIS CHAPTER ***

stopped on or close to Nopal Road. I would not have missed the presence of such a vehicle as I drove south on this moonlit night.

5) The distance between my location at the locked gate and the calculated location of this ML was 5.4 miles (**Map 9**). I was using a five-inch Schmidt Cassegrain telescope with a 1250 mm focal length as lens for my Canon Digital SLR camera. This instrument is fully capable of detecting a vehicle at that range. There was not a vehicle on Nopal Road.

Could this ML have been only a night mirage? It is not likely. When mirage conditions prevail, lights become elongated in the vertical and/or mirage images stack in the vertical. There was no evidence indicating mirage conditions. Lights were not elongated and did not repeat in the vertical. Moreover, mirages do not leave residual magnetic disturbances.

October 19, 2006: Red October

This would be one of the best nights ever for capturing informative photographs of ML behavior. Seeking closer ML encounters, my wife Sandra and I were observing from a location deep within southeast Mitchell Flat, beyond the locked gate (with appropriate permissions). We were lucky enough to see and photograph fascinating ML displays using a Canon 300D DSLR camera that had been specially modified to enable infrared (IR) frequencies.

There was a reason for that modification. With five years of experience, I had become good at sorting out MLs from vehicle headlights, ranch houses and other explainable light sources. One feature I had learned to look for were lights that repeatedly turned Off and then back On again. This was a consistent ML attribute. Interestingly, on occasions when my cameras managed to capture light tracks that included one or more Off states, the "back-on" state would appear perfectly in line with the light track before the gap. Not only in perfect alignment, but also right on time, suggesting that something unseen was moving through that visual gap in the light track. **Figure 28** is a prime example. I know from background mesas that ML 05082003 followed a rising trajectory and was at least 250 - 300 feet above local terrain with no possibility that an obstruction could account for the gap. **Figure 28** includes a significant gap caused by a period of time when the ML was in an Off state. When the light reappeared, trajectory direction, location and time were exactly the same as they would have been if the light had not gone out. Intrigued by this ML behavior, I was hoping to identify what was traveling unseen through the gap by capturing the ML's infrared signature

This modified Canon camera went on to be the camera of choice for some of my best ML photographs, including the previously reported ML event on August 11, 2006 plus October 19, 2006 and a number of others. **Being able to capture infrared (IR) frequencies did not make gaps in ML light tracks go away or expose MLs in an Off state, but it did provide evidence of ML heat emission in some cases. More than that, when MLs would slow and/or hover over a particular location, heat emitted by them would sometimes result in infrared illumination of brush below the slow moving or stationary ML. This was evidence that MLs events are in the air and generating a lot of heat. Also, explosive bursts would sometimes result in red (heated) atmospheric extensions that, unlike MLs, were wind responsive.**

All of the above effects were seen and photographically captured on the night of October 19, 2006. I sometimes refer to this eventful night as "Red October" because it occurred in October and many of the pictures have reddish coloring because they were taken with this uniquely modified Canon camera. That night I took 152 ML photographs of one very interesting ML. Many of them were repetitive, especially when the ML was moving rapidly. The important thing for readers is to see how this ML pulsed as it moved with contractions to states of small illumination followed by explosive expansions. These contraction/expansion cycles continued during the ML's lifetime. Vivid camera images collected this night convey the unique character of MLs. They are inherently dynamic

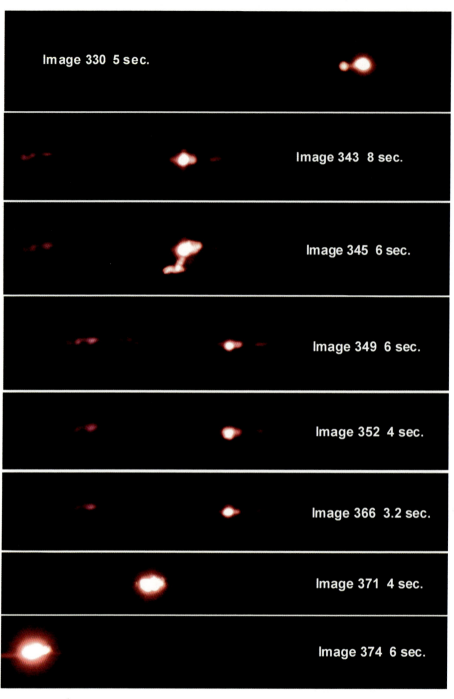

Figure 38. Eight sequential Canon infrared images taken on Oct. 19, 2006 show the ML's initial patterns of behavior. Dark night precluded capture of background terrain.

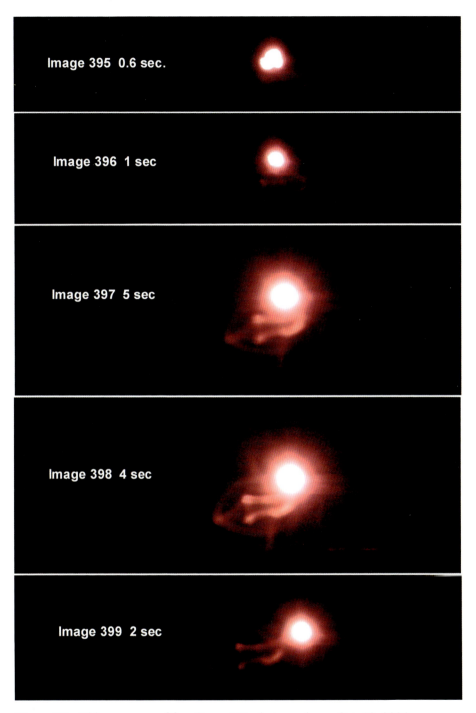

Figure 39. This sequence of five Canon ML photographs on Oct. 19, 2006 were taken a little later in time. Heat trails below the ML look like "legs." They appear to be moving left with the wind.

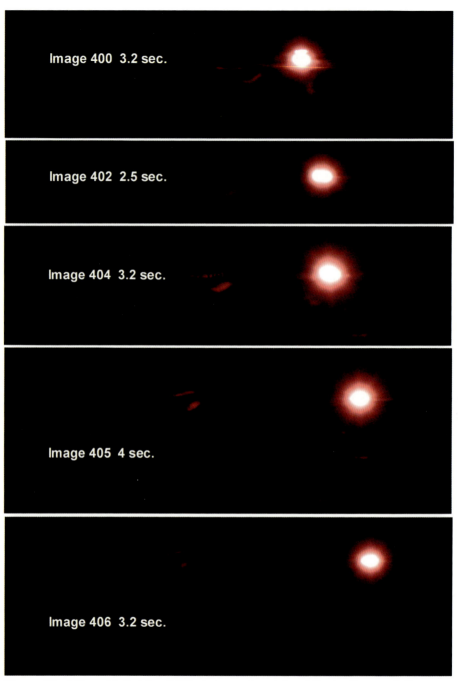

Figure 40. ML on 19 October 2006 starts moving right while the "heat trails" continue being blown by the wind to the left. Even though the ML is located above terrain "in the wind," it moves right into the wind as if the wind is not present.

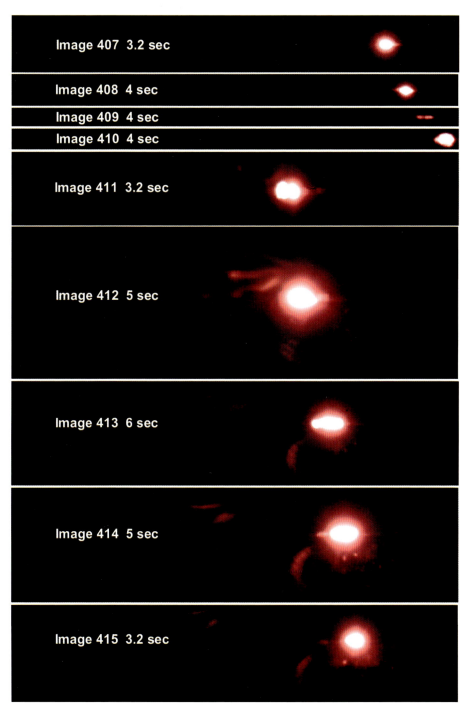

Figure 41. This sequence shows new "leg" patterns, now at the top instead of the bottom. ML goes right, slows, and expands. What may be indications of ejected materials can be seen in the last four photos.

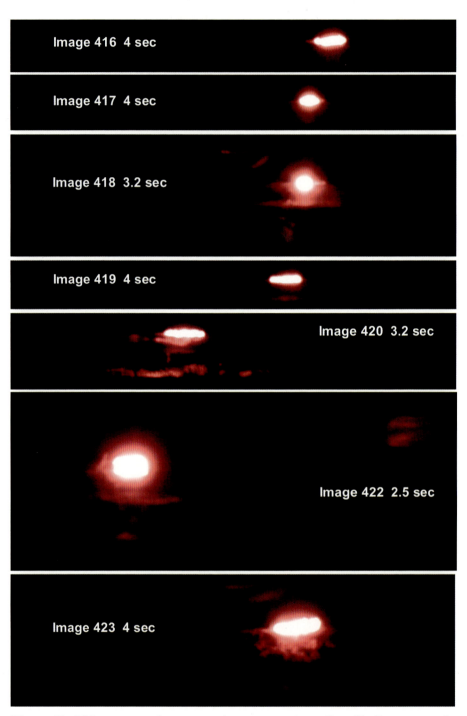

Figure 42. This sequence shows a couple more attempts to form "leg" patterns at the top. ML goes left faster, expands, and then moves rapidly back to the right. There is evidence of heating to surrounding air and brush.

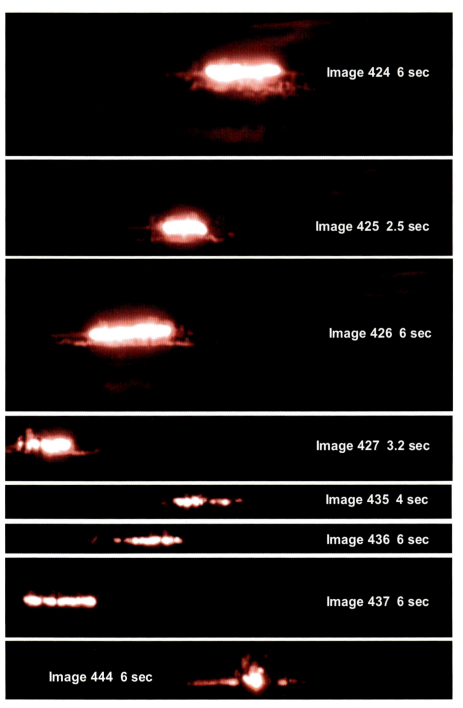

Figure 43. Eight more photographs illustrate the final sequence of patterns showing left/right movement along with more indication that it is heating surrounding air and possibly brush below the ML.

events.

A representative collection of what happened that night is presented in six composite photographs, **Figure 38 - 43**. Each composite figure is a mix of selected individual pictures cropped to save space while including all detail and presented in the order they were taken. Each image carries a sequence number and exposure time. Missing sequence numbers show where images were omitted when assembling the composite. Exposure times provide some idea of how light intensity varied over time. Elongated ML patterns in **Figure 43** were caused by ML movement while the camera shutter was open. The entire ML event lasted 21 minutes and 49 seconds. I was so busy attending to the infrared capable camera that I never managed to get the non-IR camera to lock-on, nor could I find time to take directional bearings. That was unfortunate because it was such a dark night that no background terrain was captured in any of the photographs.

While I was working feverishly to keep the camera running, Sandra found an opportunity to observe the ML using an optical telescope. She expressed amazement at what she was seeing, reporting that the center of the ML looked like a "ball of active flames." The internal action she described was not captured with any of my photographs, but is consistent with observations made by Dirk Vander Zee regarding his 1996 ML experience (HML Story #7) when he commented, **"...and they were performing some sort of internal movement, best described as multi-spectrum light folding in on itself, spherically shaped."**

Location of this ML's ground track was limited by circumstances. Automated night camera Owlbert A should have provided accurate directional information but, as luck would have it, the best located camera at Owlbert A was down that night and took no pictures. None of the other Owlbert A or Owlbert B cameras were pointed in the right direction. Roofus was also looking the wrong way but, fortunately, one other automated station, Snoopy (**Figure 44**), was working and did record the entire event.

Figure 44. Automated monitoring station Snoopy was a self-sufficient power generation station with four solar cells and a wind generator.

Image Comments

The most striking feature of this series of photographs (**Figures 38** through **43**) is how light and heat (i.e.,energy) cycled repeatedly. The reddish "something" left and right of the ML are believed to be heated air that is being blown away by wind. This fades and goes out as they cool. Saved images show repeating periods of expansion and contraction, of flaring to brightness and dimming. I believe that these variations in intensity correspond to energy consumption rates. Bright, expanding images suggest high rates of energy consumption while low intensity displays suggest reduced rates of energy consumption. ML displays often cycle from intense brightness to less intense states and back again. Periodically they go out altogether for a period of time, and then return with renewed brightness. How are they able to repeatedly restore themselves? What is the source of that renewed energy? There is no evidence of energy streaming out of the ground or descending out of the sky. Understanding the source and nature of these energy cycles is key to understanding MLs and will be discussed in more detail later.

Had I been using a recording light meter, it might have provided additional information with regard to observed energy cycles. I did not have such a meter, but was operating the Canon camera in Aperture-Priority Mode so that the camera was controlling exposure times based on available light. On a dark night with no other light sources, exposure time data is an indication of ML light intensity because as ML intensity increases, the camera automatically decreases exposure time and vice-versa. This effect can be seen (sometimes inconsistently because, in some cases, a low intensity period may be followed by a sudden flare, resulting in long exposure time associated with a large light) in these photographic reproductions. It is reasonable to expect that ML light intensity corresponds to ML energy being expended in creating visual displays.

Camera-selected exposure times varied from a low of 0.6 seconds to a high of 8 seconds and are inversely related to ML intensity. In order to display increasing intensity with increasing values, I chose to plot exposure times subtracted from the maximum exposure, eight seconds (**Figure 45**). Absolute ML intensity and energy consumption is not known, but **Figure 45** is useful in a relative sense.

Not all of the 152 images had useful data as the ML would sometimes travel out of the camera's field of view. **Figure 45** includes exposure data from 109 saved images. This figure illustrates that the ML light intensity varied throughout the ML's lifetime. Interestingly, the linear average line shows that, in this case, average display intensity was increasing over time instead of decreasing as one might expect. The bottom line with regard to **Figure 45** is simply that it shows this ML exhibited cyclical light intensity and I conclude that expended energy was also cyclical throughout the ML's life time.

Thanks to Snoopy's data, and knowing our observation location, it is possible to provide general location information as presented in **Map 10**. Interestingly, the uncertainty ellipse (see Appendix for definition) shown

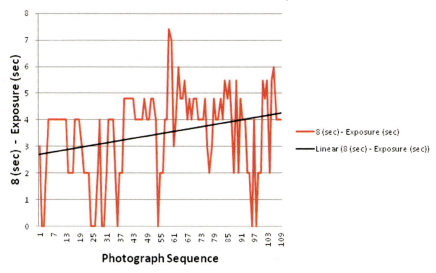

Figure 45. Camera-selected exposure times indicate that ML display intensity on October 19, 2006 cycled repeatedly, suggesting that ML energy expenditures were also cyclical.

in **Map 10** is parallel with and almost directly on top of the Walnut Creek fault line (see **Map 3**).

10/19/2006 Details

Sunset (PM CST):	7:21
Moon:	Not up - very dark night
ML duration:	00:21:49
Start (PM CST):	07:36:08
Directions from View Park:	160 deg. magnetic
Distance from View Park:	~ 13 miles
Camera location:	N30 deg. 8.901 min, W103 deg. 53.582 min.
Cameras:	Canon 300D with infrared filter removed
Camera lenses:	Celestron C5 Schmidt-Cassegrain
Automated camera:	Snoopy used for triangulation and event times

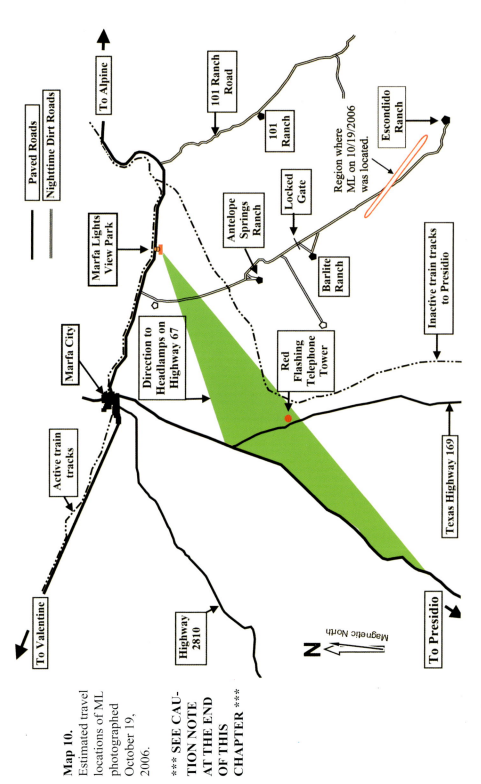

Map 10. Estimated travel locations of ML photographed October 19, 2006.

*** SEE CAUTION NOTE AT THE END OF THIS CHAPTER ***

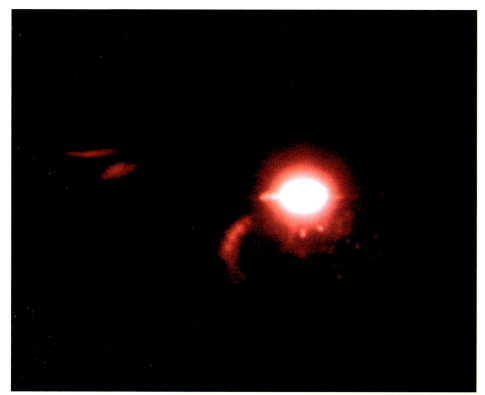

Figure 46. This expanded view of image 414 shows the shower of ejected particles in greater detail. Small groups of heated air can be seen moving left with the prevailing west wind, while the ML continues moving right into the wind. I postulate that all MLs have an intensely burning center region where plasma is converting into flammable gas and combining with atmospheric oxygen as will be discussed in Chapter 7. These central flames are not visible in any of my photographs because the process is intensely bright.

Temp. at start: 55.4 deg. F.
Humidity: 44%
Precipitation: None
Wind direction: W
Wind speed: 10.4 mph
Visibility: 10 miles

July 23, 2007: A Wild Flight

On this night the infrared capable Canon DSLR would once again record behavior of an interesting ML that lasted 22 minutes and 38 seconds. The ML appeared at 9:26:10 PM CDT on a bearing of 152.4 degrees magnetic from my location in the SW corner of the Marfa Lights View Park. This ML was too far north to be seen and recorded by any of my automated night cameras, so the actual distance from the View Park is unknown.

The complete photo sequence is 63 images long. Thirty-nine of those images are presented in **Figures 47 - 50. Figure 47** is a composite of the first ten images that shows how the ML started by moving right slowly and then began to accelerate and disappeared behind terrain consistent with flight at a low level altitude. The ML reappeared from behind terrain and was captured by image 643 (sequence **Figure 48**) at 9:41:20 PM CDT, fifteen minutes after ML start. Increasing ML intensity at this time resulted in a short 2.5 second exposure causing the photographic image to be dark. Image 644 was similar but with a longer 4-second exposure. Then something unusual happened with the next 2.5-second image, No. 645. This ML image is small but clearly shows ejected material that appears to be orbiting, or attempting to orbit, the ML center.

Image 647 shows the ML expanding and then starting to resume flight to the right at 9:42:00 PM CDT. Six seconds later Image 648 shows the ML becoming smaller and a little more elongated as it moves to the right. At 9:43:22 PM CDT, Image 653, the ML is starting to accelerate as it continues moving right. Six seconds later (Image 654) the ML is moving faster and creating an elongated light track during this five-second exposure.

At 9:44:04 PM CDT, the ML is still moving right but then reverses direction and moves left for a short time (Image 656, sequence **Figure 49**).

By 9:44:18 PM CDT (Image 657), the ML is once again moving right and traveling at greater speed as reflected in a longer light track. These elongated light tracks are repeated for the next few images until the ML goes out for about a minute. It reappears as a stationary sphere (Image 666) and holds that stationary configuration through Image 668).

Image 669 (also presented as **Figure 52**) captures a remarkable ML event at 9:45:44 PM CDT when ejected material creates a twisted light trail streaming out to the left. This photograph of ejected material provides dramatic evidence that sometimes violent processes are occurring at ML centers. [Because this particular image is such a prime example of ML behaviors, I elected to use it as cover art for the second printing of ***Hunting Marfa Lights***, in December 2009.] Fifty seconds later, Image 670 shows a more intensely red ML leaving an uneven light trail as it moves left. It then goes out for about a minute. Image 678 at 9:47:46 PM CDT shows an expanded ML starting to move left. The next two images show the ML is becoming less intense and pulsing as it continues moving left.

The fourth sequence in **Figure 50** shows the three final collected images. In Image 681 the ML is bright and still moving left. By 9:48:44 PM CDT, Image 682 captures the ML as it slows to a stop and grows in size and intensity. Image 683 at 9:48:48 PM CDT shows the final configuration as the ML burns remaining fuel and goes out. The final location is at a magnetic bearing of approximately 215 degrees from my location at the southwest View Park Plaque.

In my experience, each night of ML displays is unique, but there are common features including On/Off display patterns with variable light intensity and configurations indicating cyclical energy patterns. From photographs of this July 23rd ML (and other MLs), it is clear that combustive violence resides at the center of MLs. **Figure 51** displays the cyclical nature of light intensity over this ML's lifetime. The trend line in this case diminishes over time instead of increasing as was the case on October 19, 2006.

Figure 47. Composite of the first ten photographs of the ML on July 23, 2007

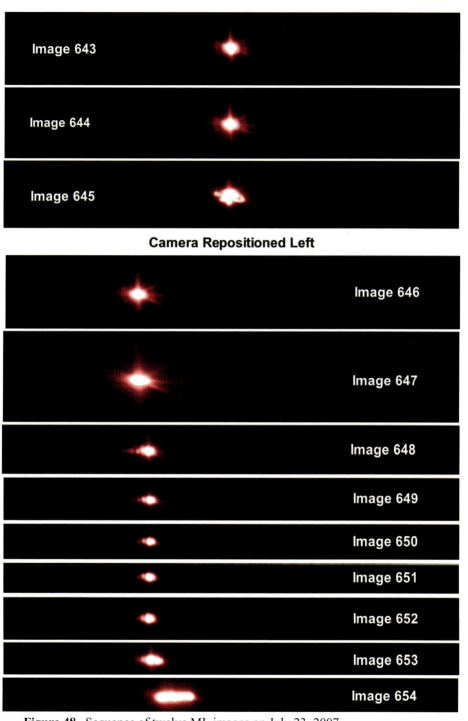

Figure 48. Sequence of twelve ML images on July 23, 2007.

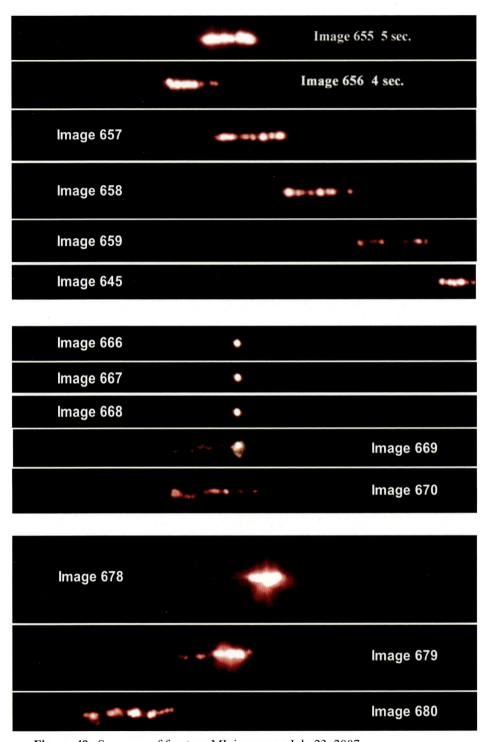

Figure 49. Sequence of fourteen ML images on July 23, 2007.

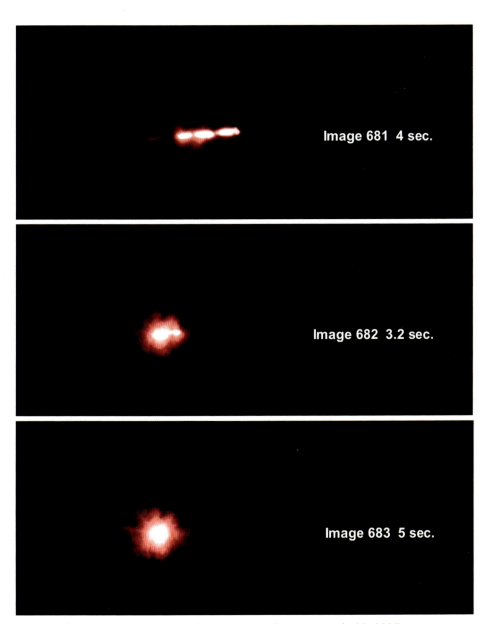

Figure 50. Sequence of the final three ML images on July 23, 2007.

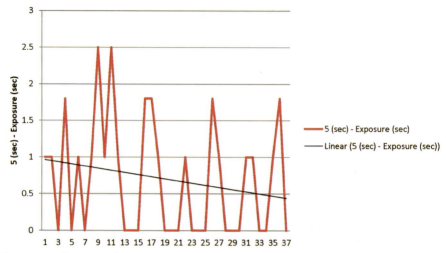

Figure 51. Camera-selected exposure times for ML23July2007 show a downward trend over the ML's lifetime. July 23, 2007 was a less dark night than October 19, 2006 resulting in reduction of maximum exposure time to 5 seconds. Consistent with the previous ML19Oct2006 chart, exposure times were subtracted from this 5 sec. max. value.

7/23/2007 Details

Sunset (CDT):	8:56 PM
Moon:	Was up
Start (CDT):	9:26:10 PM
Duration:	22' 38"
Camera location:	N30 deg. 16.499 min, W103 deg. 53.067 min.
Cameras:	Canon 300D with IR filter removed
Camera lenses:	Celestron C5 Schmidt-Cassegrain
Automated camera:	ML was too far north to be seen.
Temp. at start:	69.8 deg. F.
Humidity:	60%
Precipitation:	None
Wind direction:	SE
Wind speed:	5.8 mph
Visibility:	10 miles

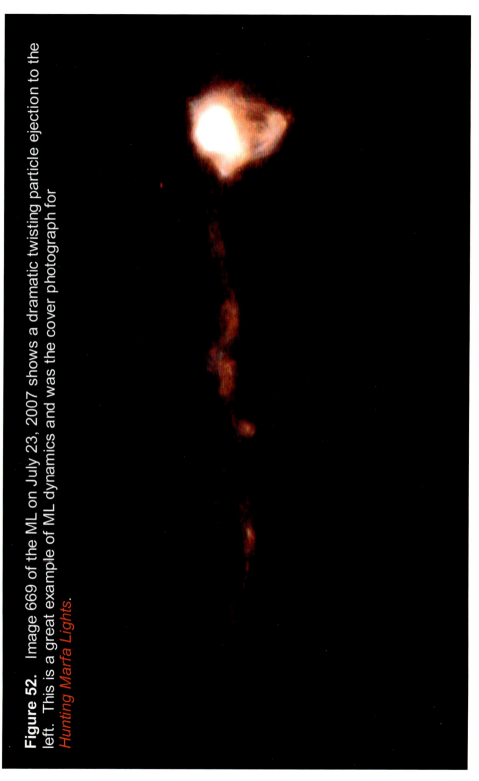

Figure 52. Image 669 of the ML on July 23, 2007 shows a dramatic twisting particle ejection to the left. This is a great example of ML dynamics and was the cover photograph for *Hunting Marfa Lights*.

*** CAUTION ***

Some readers may feel tempted to visit ML locations identified in this chapter by directional vectors and maps, or to travel down ranch roads in hopes of getting closer to MLs. Please resist these temptations for the following reasons:

1. **Every ML location identified in this book resides on private ranch property and trespassing is illegal in Texas. Ranchers can, and will, call law enforcement or Border Patrol officers. NEVER trespass on private ranch property.**

2. **One of the questions people often ask, "Has anyone ever figured out where these things are coming from and visited the location to see what is there?" Points of origin are seldom ever the same but thanks to multiple camera stations that enabled triangulation calculations, and with permission to be on ranch land at computed locations, I have searched for surface clues and have found none. My theory, as explained in this book, is that MLs are being generated by lightning deep underground and they do not produce visible displays until they have surfaced into the atmosphere where they combine/combust with oxygen to produce the displays we see and call MLs.**

3. **Please DO NOT venture down Nopal or 101 ranch roads in hopes of getting closer to the action. The Marfa Lights View Park is a better place to look for MLs. The View Park improves your chance of seeing MLs by providing the broadest possible views. Readers who ignore this advice, and venture down Nopal Road anyway, risk being stopped and searched by US Border Patrol agents whose job it is to watch for potentially illegal border traffic.**

Chapter 7
WHAT Are Those Lights?

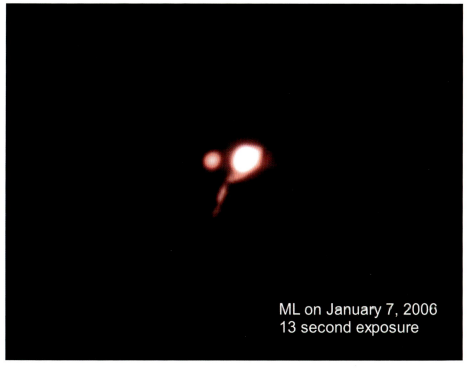

Figure 53. ML on Jan. 7, 2006 lasted 26 minutes. This 13 second exposure was the 9th frame out of 14 taken that night.

When writing ***Hunting Marfa Lights***, published in 2009, I reported ML sightings from my investigation and from the collected observations of others who shared my interest in these lights. During the final three years of my investigation, and since, I have gradually evolved a new hypothesis about the nature of MLs. My thinking has been driven by two factors: (1) MLs do not appear everywhere; the terrain probably has unique characteristics that facilitate or produce these lights. (2) MLs have characteristics in common with other natural phenomena and may be a related form of already-known, but still mysterious, Ball Lightning (BL). In this chapter I will build my case for this new hypothesis.

What is unique about the geology of regions where MLs are seen?

There may be reason to believe that MLs occur worldwide in regions with high tectonic stress. The earth's crust is broken into 17 major tectonic plates that float on the hotter earth's mantle (a subsurface layer of molten matter approximately 2100 miles deep that surrounds the earth's core (*McGraw-Hill Dictionary of Scientific and Technical Terms*)). The current geological concept is that these plates are continually moving in one direction or another while bumping and colliding with each other (McGookey, 2004). Collisions and movement of the plates subjects them to stress, resulting in earthquakes and volcanos in various locations around the globe.

The state of Texas is geologically complex. The South American-African plate, pushing on the North American plate, has buried a Texas mountain range and created a zone of compression known as the Ouachita Trend. This zone takes a sweeping S-curved path through the state, from Dallas to Austin to San Antonio, and on to the Big Bend in southwest Texas. The Big Bend region of Texas, where Marfa and MLs are located, includes a region of overthrust, the Marathon Uplift, where part of the North American plate, because of the Ouachita Trend, rides over another part, the Diablo Shelf, to create the Marfa Basin (McGookey, 2004). When subducted terrain, in this case the Diablo shelf, is thrust down into

Figure 54. Paisano Peak, feeder pipe of the volcano, is located 6.7 miles from the View Park Pavilion on a bearing of 64 degrees magnetic. US 90 from Marfa to Alpine passes through the caldera and within 4,450 feet of Paisano Peak. Chinati Mountain, another ancient volcano, is larger and further away at 42 miles on a bearing of 231 degrees magnetic from the View Park.

the mantle, it melts to create volcanos and igneous deposits in the overlying plate (http://www.en.wikipedia.org/wiki/Volcano). This is thought to be what happened in the Big Bend region of Texas around 35 million years ago. Today there are no active volcanos near the Marfa Basin, but there are a number of ancient volcanos in the Big Bend region. Two dormant volcanos located close to Mitchell Flat are Paisano (**Figure 54**) and Chinati (see **Figure 8**). When these volcanos were active, they covered the entire region with a thick layer of volcanic materials. The nearby Paisano volcano deposited extensive igneous matter, including rhyolite lava, a variety of other lava types, and welded tuff (*Geologic Atlas of Texas-Fort Stockton, 1995*).

Past and Ongoing Tectonic Stress: Wrench Faults

In addition to readily-recognized markers (e.g., mountains and extinct volcanos), tectonic stress caused by the juxtaposition and movement of major tectonic plates has produced a "wrenching" effect in the North American plate, creating a myriad of lengthy topological depressions running from northwest to southeast across Texas. These are called "lineaments" or "wrench faults." The "Texas Lineament" runs from El Paso and passes through six West Texas counties before passing into Mexico (Bolden, 1984). It cuts through the northeast corner of Presidio County, passing just north of the Marfa Lights View Park, and runs roughly parallel to the Walnut Creek Fault. Both the Walnut Creek and the Texas Lineament are wrench faults, indicators of both past and ongoing tectonic stress in Mitchell Flat. The MLs discussed in Chapter 6 (Best Evidence) were all observed in locations near Walnut Creek and related faults (**Map 3**).

Other Worldwide Locations

MLs are by no means limited to West Texas; they do occur worldwide and are known by many different names, including "Earth Lights, Ghost Lights, and Spook Lights." Chapter 5, *FAQs*, provides sources of information about these lights and their locations. Two well-known "lights" locations are Hessdalen in Norway and the Taro River Valley in Italy. Hessdalen, Norway, is located at a safe distance from an active tectonic border, but it is still one of the most active areas in Northern Europe when it comes to earthquake activity (http://www.kriseinfo.no/en/Natural/Earthquakes/Earthquakes-in-Norway/). This may be, in part, related to the active offshore volcanic activity in Norway's seas. Every year several earthquakes occur in Norway and adjacent areas, so it is probably safe to conclude that the region is subject to tectonic stress.

In April, 2010, I gave a presentation on Marfa Lights at an Earth Light conference in Fornovo di Taro, Italy. The occasion gave me an opportunity to meet two outstanding Italian ML researchers, Dr. Valentino Straser, a geologist/physicist and Dr. Massimo Teodorani, an astrophysicist. Dr. Teodorani has studied MLs (aka Earth Lights) phenomena extensively and is the author of numerous scientific papers on the subject (e.g., Teodorani, 2004, 2010). Dr. Teodorani, who is widely known for his Hessdalen research, is an expert on spectral analysis of MLs. Dr. Straser has also published numerous scientific papers regarding ML behaviors (e.g., Straser 2007, 2009). Dr. Straser was the first to suggest that ML appearances in the Taro River Valley could be predictors of earthquakes. To the extent that the prediction holds, Dr. Straser's work indicates a connection between MLs and tectonic stress since earthquakes are a product of plate movements.

Underground Lightning?

Given a relationship between MLs and tectonic stress, I found the work of Dr. Friedemann T. Freund, a NASA Earth Scientist, to be a potential key to an explanation of the source of ML energy. Dr. Freund has shown that igneous rock, when subjected to sufficient stress, starts to acquire electrical charges. When certain types of rocks are subjected to extreme stress, they can accumulate very large electrical charges, a phenomenon that Dr. Freund has demonstrated in his laboratory (*Freund, Takeuchi, and Lau, 2006*). Implications of his discovery could be very significant if extended to large underground masses of rock. When subjected to tectonic stress, underground rocks may collect electrical charges and, as do batteries and storm clouds, release those charges as conditions permit. Electrical charges generated by thunderstorms result in lightning, and I suspect that stress-generated electrical charges in igneous rocks may also have the capacity to produce lightning. If so, then underground lightning that shreds molecular and atomic structures could create "dusty" plasma "clusters." These plasma clusters could then migrate to the surface to create MLs near Marfa, as well as in similar regions of tectonic stress around the globe.

What is Plasma?

Plasma is a fundamental state of matter. We are all aware of the first three states of matter, solid, liquid and gas. Plasma is the fourth state, and because stars are plasma, it is the most common form of matter in the universe.

How does plasma differ from the other three states? As you may already know, it is possible to transition from a solid state to liquid and on to a gaseous state by adding heat. A plasma state can also be achieved by extreme heating of gas, or by subjecting matter to a strong electromagnetic field induced by, I am suggesting, underground lightning. Plasma is created when molecular and atomic structures break apart resulting in remnants of atoms in the form of positive ions and electrons moving independently of each other while maintaining an electrical balance. These swirling, charged particles generate strong electric and magnetic fields that help hold the swarm together and influence the plasma's behavior. Plasmas are able to exhibit a bewildering variety of complex behaviors including extreme sensitivity to magnetic fields, with a predilection to orbit or spiral within these fields. Lights that are plasma have distinct "discontinuous" spectra, in contrast to "continuous" spectra of non-plasma light.

Free (naturally occurring) plasma may be common in the universe, but is uncommon on earth. We are all familiar with man-made plasma devices (e.g., sodium vapor street lights, neon signs, fluorescent lights and TV displays) where we use electricity within a sealed glass tube to excite photon-emitting plasma states in a controlled way. In the case of these man-made display lights, plasma is isolated from atmospheric oxygen, or moisture, and exhibits predictable response to application of electric current causing photons to be emitted or to stop emitting when the current is applied or terminated with a light switch. Our experience with free-natural plasma is more limited. Ball Lightning (BL) is one example of natural plasma on earth.

What is Ball Lightning?

BL has been studied for years by science but is still not fully understood, partly because of its rarity. Many theories have been proposed to explain BL. The most popular current theory was proposed by John Abrahamson and James Dinniss of the University of Canterbury in Christchurch, New Zealand. They suggested that when lightning strikes the ground, it can vaporize silica-rich soil sending it into the air where it combines with atmospheric oxygen and burns in a chemical oxidation process to create BL (Abrahamson and Dinniss, 2000). Laboratory tests suggested that their theory might be valid, and then, in 2012, a team from Northwestern University of China, while photographing lightning, managed to capture possible BL spectra that resulted from a cloud to ground strike (Jianyong, Ping, and Simin, 2014). Associated with the strike was a glowing ball of light that rose about five meters into the air. Spectra from this event were discontinuous, indicating plasma, and are available online at http://en.wikipedia.org/wiki/File:Ball_lightning_spectrum.svg. It contains emission lines from silicon, iron, and calcium -- all elements expected to be in the soil. Duration of the event was less than two seconds.

BLs and MLs compared

If BLs and MLs are both products of electrical discharges and they both involve plasma, might they be two aspects of the same phenomena? The source for the following BL information is the *Handbook of Atmospheric Electrodynamics,* Volume I (Volland, ed., 1995). ML information is from the author's investigation reported in **Hunting Marfa Lights** and various ML stories.

Table 1. Comparison of BL and ML

Characteristic	BL	ML
Colors -- in order of frequency	Yellow, White, Red, Orange, Blue/Violet, Mixture, Green	White, Yellow, Red, Orange, Green, blue (Mixture in most cases)
Size	Mean = 20 cm Maximum = 110 cm	Softball (10 cm) to Basketball (25 cm)
Duration	Mean = 5 sec. Maximum = 23 sec.	Mean = 4 min. 10% > 40 min.
Multiple Displays?	No, burns once	Multiple On/Off states
First Appearance	Often near impact point of cloud-to-ground flash	Can be close to ground, above horizon or high in the sky
Odd Behaviors	BLs do not follow wind direction. Frequently observed passing through doors, windows, and into aircraft	No wind response No reports of sound

Table 1 shows considerable similarity between BL and ML events with the principal differences having to do with lifetimes (duration) and the fact that MLs nearly always turn On/Off while `BLs extinguish only once. What might account for these differences?

Plasma Physics

Plasma properties, unlike those of other states, include a wide range of characteristics as a function of temperature and particle density. Plasmas are, by their very nature, hot because high temperatures are usually needed to sustain ionization (http://en.wikipedia.org/wiki/Plasma_(physics)). Like gas, plasma tends to expand to fill any container.

At atmospheric pressure, thermal-dominate plasma is unstable. It expands explosively with lifetimes measured in milliseconds. The last section in Chapter 2, *"Look Up...,"* described lights that seemed to be exploding high in the sky, almost directly overhead. Plasma with density much less than the atmosphere would probably shoot high in the sky, expand explosively and go out quickly, but most MLs I have observed, and photographed, have had significantly different characteristics. Instead of shooting high into the sky and bursting explosively, they are usually seen, and photographed, flying low, parallel to the ground, repeatedly turning On/Off, and having long lifetimes.

The ability of MLs to fly horizontally close to the ground with long lifetimes implies that they are stable and have high particle density equal to or greater than the atmosphere. But not all MLs are low fliers. Chapter 1 includes stories of MLs performing in the sky well above the horizon. Chapter 6 details behavior of an ML(1a) on May 8, 2003 that flew a rising trajectory and then came apart explosively (**Figures 28** and **29**). These observations suggest that, if MLs are fundamentally plasma, then they probably have particle density approximately equal to, and sometimes more or less than, atmospheric density.

If low-flying MLs are denser than the atmosphere they are flying in, what would keep them from falling to the earth? The possible answer is that they are prevented from descending by a plasma-generated magnetic field that helps contain them. ML remnants are seen falling to earth as they exhaust their energy.

The bigger question, "Is is possible for naturally occurring plasma to have particle density approximately equal to, or greater than, atmospheric density while remaining stable, with long lifetimes, as ML behaviors seem to suggest?" There does exist a corner of the plasma temperature/particle-density envelope that may accommodate sufficient particle density. It is a plasma regime with relatively low temperatures and high particle densities. For plasma to even exist in this regime requires ion pairs to be strongly-coupled (Murillo, 2004). Strongly-coupled plasma has characteristics of almost continuous electrostatic influence and is considered to be cold and dense (http://en.wilipedia.org/wiki/Plasma_parameter). It should be noted that strongly-coupled plasma may be cold relative to other plasma forms, but is still well in excess of a thousand degrees Fahrenheit (i.e., above the auto-ignition temperature of hydrogen).

My hypothesis assumes that MLs are being generated deep underground by powerful electrical discharges (underground lightning). I know from many wildcat wells drilled in Mitchell Flat that hydrocarbons exist deep under Mitchell Flat and I have witnessed at least one exploratory well burning natural gas that the well had tapped into. Logically, powerful underground electrical discharges may shatter not only hydrocarbon molecules, but any elements in the discharge path, resulting in "dusty plasma." Dusty plasmas have at least three components: electrons, ions, and dust (Piel and Melzer, 2002). The dust particles are orders of magnitudes larger than the electrons and ions. The presence of these dust particles may be the source of colors seen in ML displays.

JB's ML Hypothesis

It seems reasonable to suspect MLs have both plasma content and related magnetic fields, because plasma is, to my thinking, the most logical source with sufficient variability to encompass the complex ML behaviors that I and others have observed and photographed. A possible indicator of plasma involvement is the post-event measurement taken with a hand meter (Chapter 6, night of August 11, 2006), suggesting that MLs may involve magnetic disturbances strong enough to linger long after the ML goes out. Elevated VLF, ELF and ULF were also detected with a hand meter following an ML event in the early morning hours of September 13, 2003 (***Hunting Marfa Lights***, page 111).

Some of the more paradoxical aspects of ML behaviors might be explained by assuming that MLs are a duality. The displays I call MLs, appear to be conventional oxidation fires (based on spectral analysis), but I suspect the energy source feeding them is plasma. ML observations suggest that a small electrostatically-coupled cluster of dusty plasma may reside at the center of each ML and may be the source of renewed energetic displays, accounting for ML longevity, repeated renewal, and unexplained ability to turn On/Off. The plasma cluster residing at the ML center is being slowly consumed by heat transfer into cold night air. Inside the cluster atomic remnants continue to swirl in plasma balance and generate electrical and magnetic fields, but along the cluster's surface, ions are cooling and starting to transform into atoms of gas. This ongoing state change from plasma back to gas is occurring at plasma temperatures, above the auto-ignition temperature of hydrogen. Atmospheric oxygen supplies the oxidizer, enabling conventional combustion to occur around the surface of the plasma cluster. This ongoing combustion may also be consuming other molecular elements in the mix of atom formations. The combustion process is conventional and emits photons we see and call MLs.

Figure 55 is an artistic attempt to provide a conceptual diagram of what may be happening in ML centers, based on common features reported in eye witness accounts. Red flames in a spherical-like arrangement at the center of an ML were observed and reported both by Dirk Vander Zee and Sandra Dees (see People Stories Chapter 1, HML #7 and #28. See also the 1988 event described by Charlotte Allen, SL #2, specifically the final stage of MLs that hovered near their parked car). It is also consistent with observed ML cyclic variability in brightness throughout ML lifetimes. **Figure 55** is intentionally asymmetric to illustrate how erupting chemical flames may eject flaming material out of the ML (as seen in some ML photographs) and may also impart propulsive forces to the ML. I suspect that this is the reason that MLs sometimes have oddly wandering flight paths (e.g., ML2 on May 7, 2003 and the ML2 on May 8, 2003) .

Why MLs have longer lifetimes than BLs

The 2012 BL (Chinese) event observed and recorded in the highlands of Tibet lasted less than two seconds (Jianyong, Ping, and Simin, 2014). Table 1 indicates that some BL events may last as long as 23

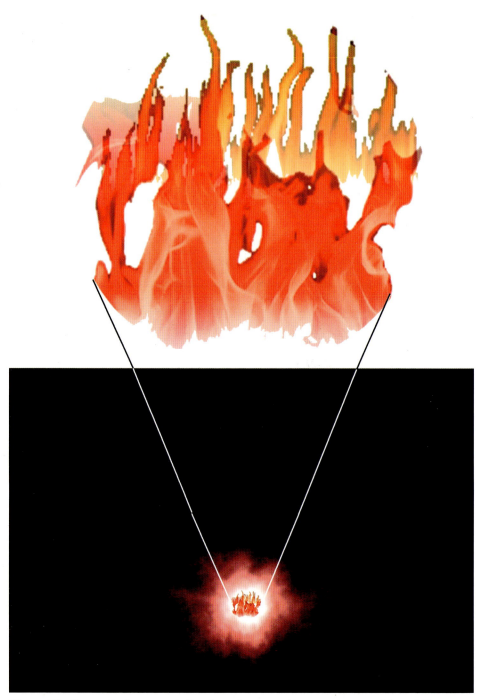

Figure 55. Conceptual representation, based on eyewitness accounts, of fiery ML centers. This would not usually be visible due to distance and extreme brightness of the ML.

Fig. 56: ML Lifecycle Cross Section

1. Altitude of the hot ML plasma cluster is a function of particle density and strength of its magnetic field. The ML radiates heat into the cold night atmosphere.

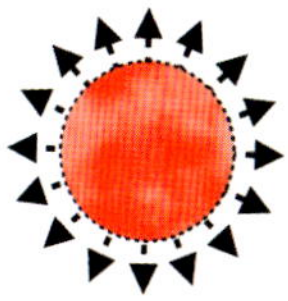

2. Low surface temperatures result in formation of atomic structures on the surface of the plasma cluster. Reconstructed hydrogen atoms immediately combine with atmospheric oxygen producing hot flames that slow the rate of heat transfer and the rate of state change.

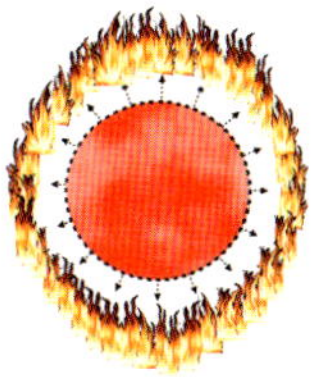

3. As surface fires grow hotter, direction of heat transfer reverses, causing state changes to cease.

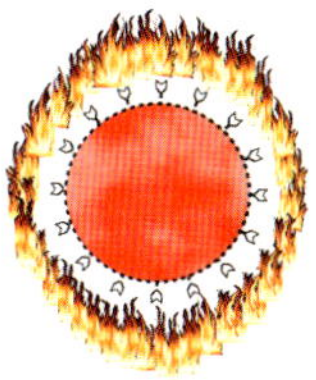

4. Surface fires exhaust available fuel and go out, causing the ML to go dark because the core cluster is dark plasma (i.e., does not emit photons).

1. With the surface fire extinguished, heat transfer from the plasma cluster accelerates resulting in more state change and auto-ignition of new surface fires. This On/Off cycle continues until the plasma cluster exhausts.

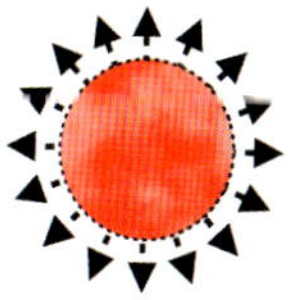

seconds. In contrast, MLs in Mitchell Flat, near Marfa, have significantly greater lifetimes (ten percent of MLs in my collection have had lifetimes greater than 40 minutes). If MLs and BLs are essentially the same phenomena, what accounts for such wide variation in recorded lifetimes and why do MLs turn On/Off repeatedly when that characteristic has not been reported for BLs?

The answer may have to do with the makeup of the pre-plasma elements. Spectra of the Chinese BL showed presence of silica and other elements from soil where the cloud to ground lightning struck. The assumption is that these reformed elements supported oxidation-combustion to produce the short-lived BL.

My working assumption for MLs is that they are driven to a plasma state deep underground in a location rich with hydrocarbons. My hypothesis is that heat transfer into much cooler night air causes reformation of atomic structures, including hydrogen, that auto-ignites in the presence of atmospheric oxygen. Resultant fires surround the plasma cluster slowing and then reversing the direction of heat transfer as illustrated in **Figure 56**. I suspect that it is chemical oxidation fires surrounding a core plasma cluster that provides the illumination we see and call MLs. Hydrogen burns clear so ML colors indicate that more than just hydrogen and oxygen are getting burned in the process. Intense heat from surrounding flames slow and, from time to time, halt state changes and cause the ML to go dark when available fuel is temporarily exhausted (**Figure 56**). When the surface fire goes out, heat transfer out of the central plasma cluster accelerates resulting in auto-ignition of a new chemical fire and this process continues until the plasma core is exhausted.

But, readers may wonder, why should MLs ever lose visibility completely as long as a hot plasma cluster still exists, and must be moving through display gaps that appear in photographs of ML light tracks? I believe the answer is that plasma does not always emit visible photons in spite of the fact that plasma is used, in today's world, to create lights and displays. Plasma has at least three different modes, dark plasma, glow plasma, and arc plasma. Proof that dark plasma exists is the simple fact that we are able to clearly see stars and planets in our night skies even though doing so requires that we look right through two thick plasma radiation belts that encircle our planet, the Inner and Outer Van Allen Belts (http://www.ibtimes.com/invisible-plasma-shield-which-protects-earth-radiation-discovered-7200-miles-above-173).

Strange Characteristic

What may make MLs terrifically important is one shockingly-odd characteristic. MLs are not wind responsive. This extremely odd characteristic is most noticeable when MLs are holding stationary positions in gusty winds. Even though they are located above ground, MLs do not appear to bob or show any wind response. When traveling cross-country they move in directions independent of prevailing winds. Assume, if you will, that propulsive forces imparted by asymmetrical chemical combustion (as described before) accounts for travel directions independent of wind forces. This still leaves unexplained their ability to hold undisturbed stationary positions in strong gusty winds.

Rest assured that I do not, even for a millisecond, believe that MLs violate laws of physics. What I believe instead is that science has not finished searching out plasma physics. People engaged in plasma research will tell you that plasma is pretty strange stuff. Could it be possible that electromagnetic attributes of ML plasma are able to influence atomic forces is some interesting ways? Perhaps an explanation of how MLs can be unresponsive to wind forces will be discovered one day in the lab by smart people engaged in plasma research. Clues I have to offer are that MLs, flying in air above Mitchell Flat, are not responding to wind or wind gusts. This astonishing behavior has been witnessed by me and others on multiple occasions (see ML Stories, Chapter 1).

Chapter 8

What Are They Not?
Marfa Night Mirages

Figure 57. Marfa city lights appear vertically elongated by mirage conditions as seen from the View Park. Night mirages are sometimes mistaken for MLs.

Any good skeptic is probably going to be tempted to suggest a simpler explanation, "MLs are only mirages." But that is not the answer. During my 12 year investigation, I have had numerous opportunities to observe both MLs and mirages; they are entirely different phenomena. Mirages do occur at night near Marfa; they are interesting and fun to watch, can be very mysterious, and even scary when they seem to chase automobiles on US 90. They are not our "mystery lights." This chapter, *Marfa Night Mirages,* provides information regarding the nature and behavior of these nighttime mirages near Marfa.

What are mirages?

A smooth water surface reflects light from a calm pool of water in a city park to show surrounding buildings and trees perfectly, but reversed. Mirages are similar reflections or refractions of light that occur when light encounters the boundary between two air masses of different temperatures and therefore different densities. People driving asphalt roads in hot weather may see a mirage-created illusion of water on the roadway ahead of them. The illusion holds until their viewing angle becomes too steep and then it disappears. This is an example of a simple mirage caused when the hot black asphalt heats a thin layer of air next to the road surface. When this happens, viewers in an approaching automobile no longer see the road surface. Instead they see light reflected from the blue sky above that looks, because it is on the ground, like water.

A hot roadway is not required to create mirages. With the right atmospheric conditions, mirages become possible, even at night. Whenever two air masses of different densities (i.e., different temperatures) are in direct contact, the boundary between them can reflect light, and that reflection can appear as a mirage. This fact of physics is significant for Mitchell Flat (where Marfa Lights sometimes appear) because Mitchell Flat is high desert (4900 feet above sea level) and surrounded by mountains. Once the sun sets, temperatures drop quickly, even in the summertime. When the wind blows, warmer air from surrounding deserts can become positioned above colder air trapped by the mountains that circle the Marfa Basin. This atmospheric condition is known as a "temperature inversion" (a "TI"). When a TI occurs, the boundary between cool air near the ground and warmer air above has potential to reflect light, creating mirages. This type of mirage is sometimes referred to as "a superior mirage" (http://en.wikipedia.org/wiki/Mirage) because light rays are reflected (bounced) upward or curved (refracted) downward. During daytime, TI mirages can create amazing illusions (that are actually reflections) of buildings, mountains, or just about anything, causing them to appear to be in locations where they are not. These false images usually appear upside down and reversed because they result from light redirected by reflection off of the boundary between two air masses with different densities.

At night, TI conditions can also create some very interesting light mirages. Although somewhat uncommon, TI atmospheric conditions do occur at night in Mitchell Flat. The first clue that TI mirage conditions prevail is the appearance of "vertical elongation" or "stacking" of lights. The elongation and/or stacking can extend either up or down with respect to the actual light location. **Figure 57** shows typical elongation of Marfa city lights as seen from the View Park. **Figure 58** shows multiple stacking of a mercury vapor ranch light. In **Figure 58,** only the top light is real. The other lights are mirage versions caused by light reflecting and/or refracting off multiple temperature/density boundaries in the atmosphere. If a temperature/density boundary in the atmosphere acts like a mirror to reflect light, then I might expect to see two lights, one real and one a mirage resulting from a reflected light path, but **Figure 58** shows multiple mirages indicating that these mirages resulted from more than reflection alone.

When light passes from one medium to another with changes in direction and wave velocity the direction change is referred to as "refraction" (*McGraw-Hill Dictionary of Scientific and Technical Terms, 1974*). A temperature inversion in the atmosphere can result in a complex type of mirage known as Fata Morgana where temperature changes with altitude

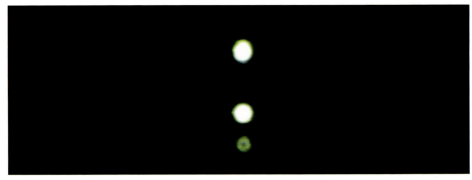

Figure 58. Mercury Vapor ranch light in mirage conditions. Only the top light is real; the other two lights are mirage copies.

can sometimes cause "tunneling of light" for long distances, including over the horizon (http://en.wikipedia.org/wiki/Mirage). That is what can happen when the boundary between two air masses is not sharply defined but is instead a temperature gradient (i.e., the gradient is variable air density created by altitude-varying temperature that makes it possible for light rays to thread through "light tunnels"). This produces complex Fata Morgana mirages as illustrated in **Figure 59**.

This chapter examines selected Marfa Lights stories and related data to assess potential for mirage phenomena as a possible explanation for unusual lights sometimes seen in the Marfa Basin.

Example Mirage Illusions

Two stories from the author's earlier book are good candidates for a mirage explanation. These are both "car chase" stories reported in *Hunting Marfa Lights* (Bunnell, 2009) and summarized below.

Chased by a White Light

This story was first reported for HML by Ms. Lydia Quiroz. Her family members added their memories of the event to the account for this book.

In March 1994, Lydia Quiroz, an Alpine bank executive, her

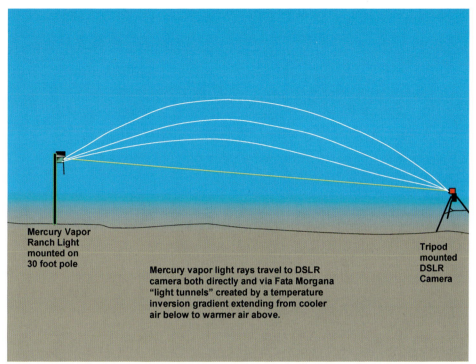

Figure 59. Illustration of Fata Morgana light tunnels causing a ranch light to appear with multiple stacked reflections.

brother, Joe Balderas, and three sisters, Maria Colfry, Sandra Aguirre and Olga Landrum, visited the Marfa Lights View Park in hope of seeing the fabled Marfa Lights. They did see unidentified lights from the View Park that may, or may not, have been MLs, but the most exciting part of their evening occurred during their return trip to Alpine. As they were driving east on US 90, Olga called their attention to a light rapidly approaching from behind and suggested that it was a Marfa Light. Joe, who was driving their car, replied that it was just a motorcycle. But as the light drew closer they could see that it was not a motorcycle. The advancing light had the shape of a vertical ellipsoid; Lydia estimated it to have been about 12 X 8 feet in size. The light was extraordinary, scintillating, and brilliant. The four passengers of the car were excited by this unexpected development and urged their brother to stop the car so they could get a closer look. He slowed the car and the approaching light slowed as well.

He then brought the car to a halt and the light also stopped an estimated 100 to 125 feet behind them. Everyone wanted to go back for a closer look, but Lydia's brother was prevented from turning because of another car approaching from the opposite direction. As the other car passed them, the driver applied his brakes sharply suggesting that he too had seen this strange light. At almost the same time, the phantom light suddenly shrank into a small irregular shape that was red in color. This red light lasted for only a brief second or two and then disappeared completely, ending their unusual encounter.

Comments:

There are important clues that point to a possible mirage explanation for this encounter.

1) The shape of the light was elongated in the vertical, a characteristic that may have resulted from a stretching of the reflected light rays in the direction of travel (i.e., the reflected image was a tilted projection of the source light).

2) The light appeared to be chasing and drawing closer to their car. This characteristic may have resulted from increasing size of the reflected light as the car moved further away from the source. As appearance of the light grew in size, it would have looked like the light was gaining on them as its apparent size was growing larger (see **Figure 60**).

3) When the car slowed, the light also slowed and then stopped when the car stopped. This is consistent with the idea that the speed and size of the light was a visual illusion created by atmospheric conditions and distance from the light source.

4) The light suddenly shrank, changed colors and then went out. Loss of the mirage could have been caused by a change in the source light or by a wind shift or atmospheric disturbance. The color change to red could have been caused by the source light, or red may have been the last visible frequency prior to the light going completely out as the mirage tunnel dissipated.

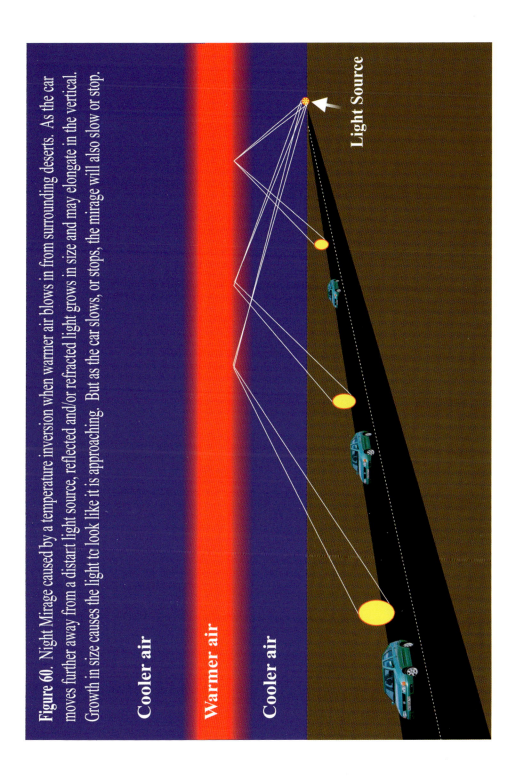

Figure 60. Night Mirage caused by a temperature inversion when warmer air blows in from surrounding deserts. As the car moves further away from a distant light source, reflected and/or refracted light grows in size and may elongate in the vertical. Growth in size causes the light to look like it is approaching. But as the car slows, or stops, the mirage will also slow or stop.

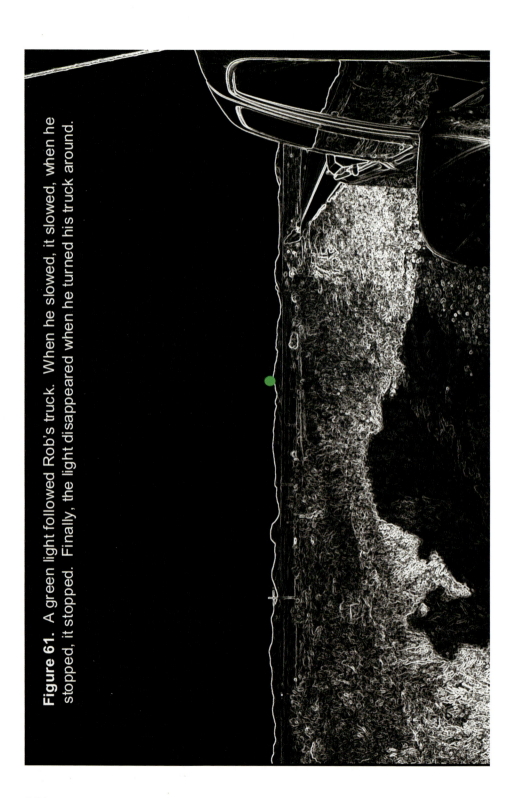

Figure 61. A green light followed Rob's truck. When he slowed, it slowed, when he stopped, it stopped. Finally, the light disappeared when he turned his truck around.

Chased by a Green Light

On August 12, 2008, at approximately 10 PM, Mr. Rob Grotty, a Forester for Texas Forest Service, was driving westbound on US 90 toward Marfa when he noticed a strange green light following him in his right rear view mirror. Turning his head and looking through the untinted glass window of his pickup he could see a ball of green light flying above nearby railroad tracks that parallel the road he was on. The light did not radiate or show evidence of a light beam. He was driving 65 mph and the light seemed to be moving a little faster than that because it was catching up to him (i.e., growing in size). With the light three or four car lengths behind him, he slowed down to allow the light to pass so that he could get a better look at it. But when he slowed, the light also slowed. Curious to know what this strange light might be, he pulled to the side of the road and stopped. To his surprise, the strange green light also stopped. Rob estimated the light was located about ten feet above the railroad tracks, higher than a similar green section light located farther down the tracks. So far as Rob could tell, the light was not attached to anything but held its position unsupported. Rob turned his truck around to drive closer to the light, but it disappeared while he was turning (**Figure 61**).

Comments:

This encounter is similar to the 2004 encounter by Lydia Quiroz and her family. It is a good candidate to have been caused by a Fata Morgana mirage for the following reasons:
1) The light did not radiate or show a light beam.
2) The light seemed to be catching up to Rob, but when he slowed and stopped, the light also slowed and stopped.
3) When Rob turned his vehicle around moving it to the other side of the road, the light disappeared. This may have resulted because Rob moved out of the Fata Morgana "light tunnel."

Mirages do not explain MLs

There is no doubt that night mirages do exist from time to time in Mitchell Flat and are, without a doubt, the source of some ML reports. The two stories sited here are good candidates for mirage explanations. However, the vast majority of ML events recorded over the last decade have exhibited characteristics that either preclude or render unlikely a mirage explanation for one or more of the following reasons:

1) Thanks to use of automated night cameras, reported MLs have been observed and/or recorded from widely separated observation view points. MLs observed from different locations involving significant angular separation are unlikely to be mirages because atmospheric conditions that enable mirages have restricted fields of view.
2) MLs operating for long time frames are unlikely to be mirages because atmospheric conditions necessary are fragile and easily disturbed by wind and/or motion of the light source.
3) Many MLs exhibit complex features and/or motions that would seem to preclude any logical source light equivalent.
4) Some MLs have been observed and/or photographed while ejecting falling components that, in turn, exhibit residual motion. Such events are inconsistent with a mirage explanation.

Chapter 9

Why Mystery Lights Are Important

At the start of my investigation in November, 2000, I was aware that the lights we had seen were out of the ordinary. They were clearly not car lights; they pulsed independently and seemed to follow a random sequence with variable brightness and intermittent off states. The duration of these lights was an extraordinary six and a half hours on 11-25-2000, far too long for fragile mirage conditions. Also, we would learn later that another observer, Sharon Eby Cornet, saw the same lights from Nopal Road, a much different viewing position from ours at the View Park. Clearly, these displays were neither mirages or car lights.

What struck me at the time was how the lights held stationary locations even though it was a windy night. This suggested to me that they were probably electric light bulbs mounted on some kind of frame to keep them above ground level. That explanation was blown away the next night. They again appeared in the same fixed locations, but were accompanied by many other lights turning on and off randomly.

That second night convinced me that these were more than electric light bulbs, but did nothing to explain how those lights were able to hover in fixed locations with no wind response. I would be reminded of that unusual characteristic again in March, 2002, when I and other View Park visitors witnessed another stationary performance with MLs holding their position in strong gusty winds (Chapter 1, HML Story 13).

Stationary displays would turn out to be rare, but there would be many other ML encounters involving complex behaviors as presented in Chapter 6. Each night seemed to be unique with different points of origin and different displays. Sometimes MLs would shuttle left and right but their overall direction, time after time, seemed to be to the northwest, basically in line with fault lines in Mitchell Flat. Some characteristics were hard to put together. Their longevity, ability to turn on and off repeatedly, to change shapes and colors and to fly close to the ground or to shoot high into the night sky, were complex characteristics pointing to plasma content, but captured spectra were consistently continuous, indicating not plasma, but chemical fires. As my investigation went forward, my curiosity grew: What in the world are these strange lights in West Texas? The more I studied the lights, the more convinced I became that, fundamentally, they must be plasma even though their spectra indicated otherwise.

There were other clues. The night of October 19, 2006, wife Sandra detected active flames at the very center of bright displays I was trying to photograph. Her discovery was not the first. Dirk and Sarah Vander Zee had reported similar observations that occurred in 1996 (HML Story 7). Then there is the remarkable story by Charlotte Allen describing the final stage of a group of five MLs that hovered near their automobile, **"As each light extinguished, individual shafts of light emanated from the center, encasing what looked like thousands of dust particles"** (SL Story 2).

The hypothesis presented in Chapter 7, *"What Are Those Lights?"* provides a logical explanation that addresses divergent ML attributes by recognizing that MLs are a duality. It is my belief that the beautiful light we see is a chemical oxidation fire fueled by, and periodically renewed by, a plasma core that functions as an energy engine, enabling multiple re-starts and long lifetimes.

As explained in Chapter 7, plasma states generate strong magnetic fields that help contain them. Evidence of an elevated magnetic disturbance was detected with a hand-held meter in the early morning hours of August 12th, approximately one hour after the August 11, 2006 ML went out, as described in Chapter 6, *"Best Evidence."* This meter reading suggests the possibility of a lingering and strong magnetic disturbance associated with that ML. Such a magnetic field may also explain the ML's ability to fly in the air close to the ground, neither touching the ground nor soaring high into the sky.

Some MLs are high flying while others travel at low altitudes near the ground. My hypothesis, as discussed in Chapter 7, attributes these divergent altitudes to variation in ML densities relative to atmospheric density. **Figure 28,** *"Best Evidence"* Chapter 6, captured an ML with a gradually rising trajectory illustrating a case when the ML was slightly more buoyant than the atmosphere it was flying in.

Photograph sequences taken on the night of October 19, 2006, Chapter 6, *"Best Evidence,"* using a camera that was capable of detecting infrared frequencies, captured elements of heated air being carried to the left by prevailing wind while the ML was moving to the right, into the wind. This interesting series of photographs also shows heating of desert brush below moving MLs. This is consistent with my hypothesis that ML displays are chemical fires erupting around a plasma core with heat transfer causing ongoing state changes (from plasma to gas).

By far the most fascinating ML observations have to do with their mysterious ability to completely ignore wind forces. A possibly related characteristic may be absence of sound. I have witnessed many of these lights and have never heard any ML sounds. Perhaps I have never been close enough to hear any sounds, but other ML witnesses have not reported sounds either, even though some of them have experienced close encounters. Could the absence of sound be a companion aspect of "no wind response?" The answer to that question is unknown.

With regard to the claim that MLs are not wind responsive: This has been my unmistakable observation (HML #10 and #13) and others have also reported this characteristic in ML stories (e.g., SL #1). I also have one case that was captured by automated monitoring station Snoopy on the night of July 30, 2008 CDT (July 31 Universal Time). At the time, this Snoopy camera was pointed 58 degrees magnetic (51 degrees true) northeast.

The ML started at 9:21:10 PM and lasted 27 min. 38 sec. I did not witness this event, but video collected by Snoopy shows the ML holding the same angular position throughout its lifetime while also turning On/Off. **Figure 62** provides a brief sampling of video frames. The actual video is a good deal more entertaining because it shows this active, stationary ML expanding and contracting in typical ML fashion. There was no wind response. The unavoidable conclusion is that something unusual and important must be happening to account for these extraordinary observations. How can MLs flying or maintaining a position in the air remain unre-

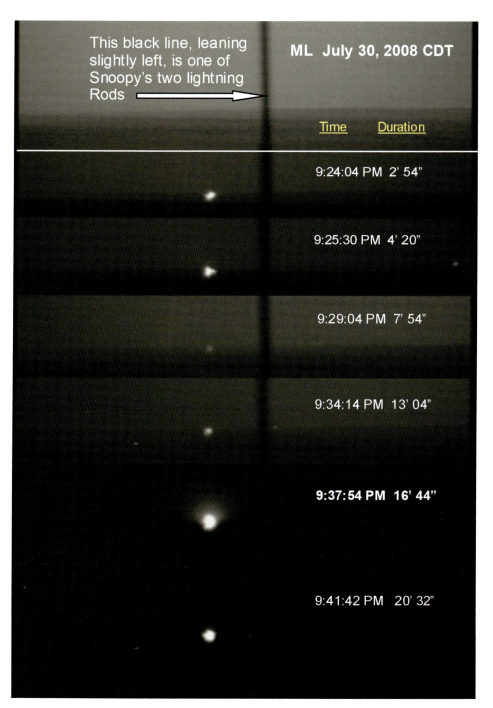

Figure 62. Sample video frames from Snoopy showing this ML holding its position throughout its 27 min. 38 sec. lifetime.

sponsive to wind pressure? The very notion that this might be happening seems impossible, but these observations are a reality. The explanation for them is an unsolved continuing mystery, too important to be ignored.

A few people who read this book will share my amazement and excitement that MLs appear to be non-responsive to wind. Many, and maybe most, readers will simply dismiss that claim immediately as impossible. I can relate to their response. It has taken me years to accept the reality and significance of these observations.

What might be the explanation? According to my theory, MLs are, at their core, concentrations of plasma that is slowly being converted into flammable gas by heat transfer. Inside the plasma core, ions and electrons swirl in some kind of balanced formation, devoid of normal atomic structure. We are tempted to speculate that this highly disturbed particle distribution has somehow opened the door to penetration by air molecules. Theoretically there should be ample space to allow such penetration because the ions, electrons, and molecules are believed to be tiny compared to their relative spacing. We can extend our speculation to assume that atomic forces that would normally prevent such intrusion are, somehow, suspended within the magnetic field being generated by the plasma. But, even if that is true, it still leaves us with ongoing chemical fires external to the plasma core. What about those chemical elements? Why wouldn't they be subject to wind pressure? Could it possibly be that whatever is happening to suspend atomic forces extends as far as the magnetic field being generated by the plasma core? I have to admit, that seems a stretch.

But the facts, as I see them, do suggest that something very unusual is happening because MLs, including both their theoretical plasma cores and surrounding chemical fires, are not wind responsive. Implications of this state of affairs are huge. Might it be possible to build a craft that can be flown thousands of miles an hour without breaking the sound barrier? Could this be the basis for technology that might explain some UFO reports? Might it explain why UFOs are sometimes tracked on radar while flying through the air at incredible speeds without breaking the sound barrier or emitting detectable sounds? We should at least, consider the possibilities.

And the next time you hear someone explaining that "Marfa Lights" are nothing more than car lights, hyped by the Marfa Chamber of Commerce to stimulate tourism, just smile and let them rant. You now have, I hope, good reason to think otherwise.

J. Bunnell, 2015

Appendix
Automated Night Cameras

Nighttime Automated Video Monitoring

As previously reported, investigation of Marfa Lights began in December, 2000, after observing extraordinary ML events during the prior month. It quickly became obvious that the principal obstacle to be overcome was infrequency of ML appearances. This was no small problem because I lived 500 miles away and was spending night after unproductive night, waiting for any ML activity and rarely finding any. The number one priority was to discover some pattern that would give me a way to predict when MLs were most likely to appear. My night camera station "Roofus" was conceived as a way to search for ML event patterns. It became operational in February 2003. The initial version was primitive, but continuing equipment upgrades and operator experience, significantly improved system results.

No event patterns emerged, but addition of a second night station, "Snoopy," opened the door to triangulation of ML locations and a few MLs were located based entirely on vectors of these two monitoring stations. Triangulation of video vectors suffered from two inherent shortcomings. Both monitoring stations were located near the west end of Mitchell Flat looking east and were less than two miles apart. This resulted in elliptical shaped areas, long in the east-west direction, where triangulated MLs might actually be located. An even bigger problem had to do with triangulation of moving targets (and they nearly always were moving). To locate the intersection of a moving ML required matching video frames of the two cameras at exactly the same time. Both recorders had uncontrolled clocks that were prone to drift, making the time match inaccurate. This problem was solved in late 2005 by extracting time from GPS satellites and adding time data as image overlays **(Figure A1)**.

Vector Directions

Automated nighttime monitoring cameras were equipped with low magnification lenses (in most cases, no magnification was used) in order to keep the field of view as wide as practical. Target angles could then be

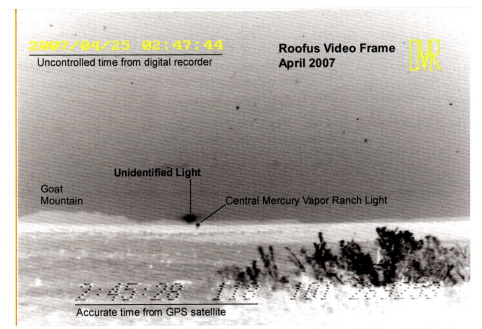

Figure A1. Video frame from Roofus shows accurate time pulled from GPS satellites versus uncontrolled digital video recorder clock time. Figure is shown as a negative to make uncontrolled time data readable.

calculated as a function of lateral displacement from known directional references. The central mercury vapor ranch light (CMV) mounted on a 28-foot pole, located at N30 deg. 08.256 min., W103 deg. 51.774 min., provided an excellent direction reference because screen measurements could be converted into corresponding angles from this reference light. The light was bright and easy to see so camera directions were oriented to include this valuable direction reference whenever possible. Other ranch lights could be used as reference points as well, and I experimented with solar powered lights mounted on fence posts. However, the fence post lights were mounted too close to the ground and were never bright enough to make good directional reference points.

Unfortunately, the CMV light eventually burned out and was not replaced. A sodium vapor light located at Barlite ranch served as a substitute directional reference for the remainder of my investigation. The south cliff end of Goat Mountain was also usable on all but the very darkest nights. In addition, the rugged mesa profile (see **Figure 12**) provided useful directional reference points for evaluating photographs and video frames taken from the View Park and other locations in Mitchell Flat.

The addition of camera stations Owlbert A and Owlbert B in 2006 greatly enhanced my ability to locate MLs and their trajectories from automated camera video. As a result, data acquisition based on automated camera data provided a more effective means of monitoring MLs on a nightly basis as well as providing location and time data for the MLs that I photographed during my trips to the area.

Computational Accuracy

Accuracy of the computed ML locations presented in Chapter 6 is dependent on 1) how many vector intersections were available, 2) accuracy of directional references, and 3) distances from each camera. These circumstances can vary and increase or decrease accuracy.

First, to compute any ML location requires an intersection of at least two directional vectors. In most cases, MLs were located by knowing direction to the ML from the point where I was photographing, and combining this with one or more directional vectors from monitoring stations that were also recording the ML. Location accuracy was enhanced whenever MLs were in view of multiple monitoring station cameras.

The second factor has to do with accuracy of the individual vectors, and the third involves distance because directional errors grow with distance. All measurements have error, and the key to understanding positional accuracy is in knowing how measurement errors combine to produce regions of uncertainty. **Figure A2** illustrates a typical example involving two different points of observation. A monitoring station camera frame that captures both the target light and a precisely known ranch light (for directional reference) might yield a directional vector accurate to within plus or minus one or two tenths of a degree. If the ML is 15 miles from Camera 1, lateral uncertainty from that monitoring station camera would be on the order of 276 to 553 feet. If the ML is also 15 miles from

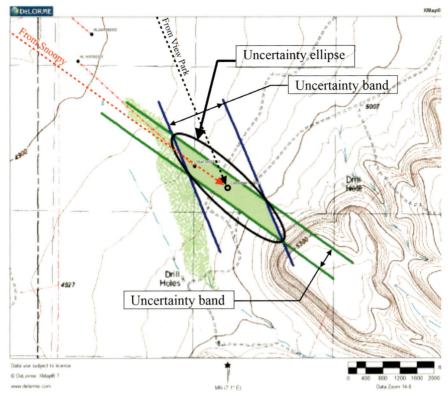

Figure A2. All measurements have error. Uncertainty envelopes vary by location depending on camera distance and available reference information as discussed in the text.

my location at the View Park and the directional reference for my tripod mounted camera at the View Park is based the background mesa profile, lateral uncertainty of that estimate might be on the order of plus or minus one half to one degree resulting in an uncertainty band width for that direction on the order of 1382 to 2764 feet. These two measurements are then combined to develop an uncertainty ellipse that encloses the two uncertainty bands as illustrated in **Figure A2.**

    The one message I hope to convey in this regard is that, even when we are dealing with small directional inaccuracies, if large distances are involved (as they are in most cases), small angular measurement errors can add up to surprisingly large areas of uncertainty. That fact complicates doing daylight searches of any computed locations. Have I ever searched

Figure A3. A second camera was added to Snoopy in 2008.

out an entire area of uncertainty looking for clues? Yes, I have done that in open pasture where I could utilize my truck in the search. No surface clues were found.

Camera Directions

As previously mentioned, camera stations Roofus and Snoopy looked eastward with Highway 67 behind them and US 90 north of their field of view. Snoopy was later given a second camera looking NE (**Figure A3**) that enabled capture of the ML shown in **Figure 62.** Night station Owlbert A and B were located beyond the locked gate with multiple cameras looking in multiple directions. Owlbert A had initial views ENE (74 deg. M), SE (138 deg. M.;2 cameras), and S (195 deg. M.). Owlbert B (**Figure A4**) had initial views E (95 deg. M.), NE (37 deg. M.) and NNW (333 deg. M.). Some of these were later redirected to investigate sectors in the direction of Marfa and to fine-tune search vectors to the southeast.

Figure A4. Owlbert B automated cameras.

Camera Types

With the addition of a second camera at Snoopy in October 2008, there were a total of ten cameras. Seven of them were Watec 120N cameras with an amazing ability to see in almost complete darkness. This was accomplished by providing users with a control box to dial in desired light gain (amplification) and to enable light accumulation by automatically stacking images. Full light gain capability of these cameras could not be used because at higher gain settings, brightness of the full moon would overwhelm everything else to create a condition known as "white-out." The most useful light gain settings did cause white-out conditions for about the first hour after sunset and during the last hour before sunrise, preventing the Watec cameras from capturing images of MLs that occurred in that time period. To provide coverage for this important time frame, Owlbert A and B were each equipped with one SuperCircuits PC164 Hi-resolution cameras capable of 0.0001 Lux. This was also a great camera, but less light sensitive than the Watec 120 N cameras. These PC164 cameras were able to record video day or night, and therefore able to cover periods when the more sensitive Watec cameras were experiencing white-out conditions. That was the reason for two Owlbert A cameras pointing in the same direction.

References

Abrahamson, J. and **Dinniss, J.** Ball lightning caused by oxidation of nanoparticle networks from normal lightning strikes on soil. *Nature* Vol. 403, 519-521, 2000.

Bolden, P. G. Wrench faulting in selected areas of the permian basin. *Transaction Southwest Section* AAPG, 1984.

Bunnell, J. *Hunting Marfa Lights.* Benbrook, Texas: Lacey Publishing Company, 2009.

Corliss, W. R. *Lightning, Auroras, Nocturnal Lights, and Related Phnomena.* Glen Arm, MD: The Sourcebook Project, 1982.

Corliss, W. R. *Remarkable Luminous Phenomena In Nature: A Catalog of Geophysical Anomalies.* Glen Arm, MD: The Sourcebook Project, 2001.

Cowley, S. C. and **Peoples, J., Jr.** Co-chairs of Plasma 2010 Committee. *Plasma Science Advancing Knowledge in the National Interest,* National Research Council, Washington, D.C.: 2010.

Freund, F. T., Takeuchi, A., and Lau, B. W. S. Electric currents streaming out of stressed igneous rocks -- A step towards under standing pre-earthquake low frequency EM emissions. *Journal of Physics and Chemistry of the Earth* (31), 2006.

Gardiner, W. B. *Structure, Subsidence and Reservoir Potential of Marfa Basin, Texas.* Amoco Production Company, 1991.

Jianyong C., Ping Y., and Simin X. Observation of the optical and spectral characteristics of ball lightning, *Physical Review Letters,* PRL 112, 035001, 17 January, 2014.

Lapedes, D. N., ed. *Dictionary of Scientific and Technical Terms.* New York, NY: McGraw Hill, 1969.

McGookey, D. P. *Geologic Wonders of West Texas.* Midland, Texas: McGookey, 2004.

Murillo, M.S. Strongly coupled plasma physics and high energy-density matter. *Physics of Plasmas,* Vol. 11, No. 5. *Amercan Institute of Physics,* DOI: 10.1063/1.1652853, 2004.

Piel, A. and Melzer, A. Dusty Plasmas -- The State of Understanding from an Experimentalist's View. *Advanced Space Resources,* Vol 29, No. 9, 1255-1264, 2002.

Stephan, K. D., Bunnell, J., Klier, J., Komala-Noor, L. Quantitative Intensity and Location Measurements of an Intense Long-Duration Luminous Object Near Marfa, Texas. *Journal of Atmospheric and Solar-Terrestrial Physics,* Vol. 73, No. 13, 1953-1958, 2011.

Straser, V. A "jackpot" for the forecast of earthquakes, the seismic swarm in the northwestern apennines. *New Concepts in Global Tectonics Newsletter,* No. 51, June, 2009.

Straser, V. Precursory luminous phenomena used for earth quake prediction -- The Taro Valley, Northwestern Apennines, Italy. *New Concepts in Global Tectonics Newsletter,* No. 44, September, 2007.

Teodorani, M. A long-term scientific survey of the Hessdalen phenomenon, *Journal of Scientific Exploration* Vol. 18, No. 2, 2004.

Teodorani, M. A scientific approach to the investigation on anomalous atmospheric light phenomena. *NARCAP Technical Reports,* 2010.

About the author

James Bunnell grew up in West Texas, graduated from Marfa High School, received his engineering degree from New Mexico State University followed by graduate work in Psychology at Georgia State University and in Aviation Systems at University of Tennessee Space Institute. James and his wife, Sandra Dees, currently reside in Fort Worth.

He is the author of three other books on Marfa Lights:
Seeing Marfa Lights, 2001
Night Orbs, 2003
Hunting Marfa Lights, 2009

James retired in 2000 after a 37 year career in the aerospace industry.

Company	Location	Assignment
LTV Systems	Dallas, TX	Systems Testing, F8, C142,
Lockheed	Marietta, GA	Value Engineering, C5, C141, C130
McDonnell Douglas	Huntington Beach	Program Office Saturn S IVB
	Kennedy Space Ctr, Fla	Program Office S-IVB
Arnold Research	Tullahoma, TN	Solid Rocket Test Management
McDonnell Douglas	St. Louis, MO	Design to Cost
	St. Louis, MO	Mission Plans Defense Analysis
General Dynamics	San Diego, CA	Program Manager MPS ARMS
GDE Systems	San Diego, CA	Program Manager MPS ARMS
Tracor	San Diego, CA	Program Manager MPS APS
BAE Systems	San Diego, CA	Director Mission Planning projects